How To Get A Job Vegas Style

Brian Waters

Copyright © 2020 by Brian Waters

All rights reserved. No part of this book may be reproduced in any manner whatsoever without written permission except in the case of brief quotations embodied in critical articles and reviews.

First Printing, 2020

For My Mom and Dad, my brothers, their wives and my nieces and nephews, Thank you for all the Love and Support. For My close friends. For Dr. Vaughan, Dr. Kung and all the medical staff at UCSD and Scripps Clinc. For the Love, Inspiration and Encouragement from the Princesa en Rosa.

CONTENTS

	DEDICATION	iii
1	Buckle Up	2
2	Oasis In The Desert	5
3	Your Vegas Guide "Phono"	9
4	The Surface Of Planet "Vegas"	14
5	Vegas Is Always Open And Changing	17
6	The Lights Of Vegas	19
7	The Action Of Vegas	32
8	What Makes Vegas-Vegas: What Makes You-YOU!	43
9	Vegas Is Selling-Everything Is Sales	49
10	A Job Is A Performance	58
11	Vegas Is A Brand: Brand=You	61

CONTENTS

- 12 | Prepare For The Vegas Performance — 69
- 13 | The Interview The Artificial Sweetener Not The Sugar — 78
- 14 | Presentation The Vegas Way — 86
- 15 | Degree Or Not Degree, That Is The Question — 88
- 16 | Planning The Vegas Adventure — 91
- 17 | Vegas is Always Changing So Should We — 94
- 18 | The Offer, The Contract — 98
- 19 | Daydreaming About Vegas — 103
- 20 | How To Get To Vegas — 112
- 21 | Playing Slots Time — 115
- ABOUT THE AUTHOR — 117

1

Buckle Up

My new morning routine after leaving Miami, now living closer to some of my family. I wake up at 5:30am and walk the one block to Starbucks through the campus of OU (Oklahoma University). I think about the world now with the epidemic of Covid 19 and how everything has changed. The local nightlife scene here with the bars, restaurants and the OU campus, is quieter now, because of these changes in our world. Recently, I have had many conversations with new graduates and some students with a year to go to completing their degree and some just starting their college adventure. There is so many unknowns for them. Are the college campuses going to open and when? Many of their lives are on hold. Our conversations then would shift to one of hope and inspiration. There are opportunities to find your career or a job that leads you to a fulfilling career and there available, even in this time of uncertainty. I can think of no better example than Las Vegas. The initial odds were against the concept of building a "Oasis" in the Mojave Desert, ironically a place where people go to gamble. The investors also had to gamble with the idea and concept of what has truly become a worldwide destination for both global business, entertainment, and vacation.

Since we are going to be on this adventure together to ride this rollercoaster of life, like at New York- New York Casio. I wish I could sit next to each of you by the Aria pool and learn about your dreams and goals.

Let me be your guide through these chapters of **"How To Get A Job Vegas Style"**. We together will see the sights of Vegas, the behind scenes of Vegas and if you are open the behind the scene of this **Production Called Life**. I always try and find the good in things, in the ebb and flow of life. The tide of life comes in and goes out. There are storms of the sea, of life and the sea is full of many unknowns. Rip currents can take us to different locations and experiences, the waves can toss you about and then in a moment the water is calm, relaxing and peaceful. The approach to **"How to Get a Job Vegas Style"** I hope you find fun, challenging, warm hearted and inspiring! If you were to interview me about what my life would look like, it would not even close to how I imagined it would be. Totally different, from the triumphs to complete and utter despair. Finding the challenge to see the good in what those around me would say is "not so good". To learn to like to be around myself when I really did not want to hang out with me at all. In this book I think you find a fresh approach and I hope you our encouraged by the words on every page. I am on the sidelines rooting for all of you, whether you are beginning of your adventures in a career. In a time of reinventing yourself or in a season of reflection and discovery or maybe even in recovery, looking for a new start. This world and the people in it can be cruel and harsh, but other people can show compassion and support infused with love. Dream big, try to strive to be better, grow! Be the best at what you do. Know your strengths and weaknesses. Find your place in the world (what are you good at). Everyone is good at something. It takes many talents to do a Vegas production, where is your contribution. It is great to try everything if you need to discover what that something is. What I have learned, is to be open. Keep your eyes wide open, your heart guarded, but still soft and to be always in **"Learn Mode"**, this has been my thought my whole life. I hope to encourage you to learn from my triumphs and my mistakes, that is why I wrote this book. I want everyone to succeed, to seek out your dreams, live your dreams and find peace and fulfillment along the way.

What is your place in this world and what is my place as well? Since most of life is work, what does your job or career look like? Yes, there is a distinction between a job and a career, we together will look at that as well. **Buckle Up** the flight into Vegas can have a lot of turbulence, but the adventure awaits when you see the **Lights on the Vegas Strip!!** Come join me at the gambling table. I am putting my chips down on you, I believe in you. I believe everyone has gifts and talents, they just need to be discovered, like this thriving place we call Las Vegas!

2

Oasis In The Desert

Who would have thought in the early 1900's, that this location in the Mojave Desert, would become the global oasis it is today? Bringing water in from the Hoover dam in the 1930's made the concept come alive. This is Las Vegas, Viva Las Vegas! Vegas encompasses, every business concept, you can imagine, and it is done with excellence and precision. This is the reason, the who's who top global companies from Enterprise, Mid-Market and Small Business, have their sales retreats and industry trade shows here. Companies have a choice and with over 6 million business and consumer attendees, that arrive in Las Vegas each year. Over 50 million flights into this desert wonderland a year and the amount that is spent by visitors each year is around 40 billion. Vegas leads the way as one of the most desirable designations for business conventions and to a top vacation- destination as well. Artists, performers, and musicians have set up residence in Las Vegas, so the fans come to see them, instead of them being on the road all the time, what a great concept. Vegas not only conceived it, but perfected it, with state-of-the-art venues, that have incredible lights and sound production! Even walking the Las Vegas strip, you will have the lights and sounds experience, everywhere you look! The show is everywhere, even all the entertainers that walk the Strip. Oh I mean the people.

It is not a new idea for this desert oasis, being a place of lights and sound, it has been from the early days beginning with the "Rat Pack". Names like Elvis Presley, Sammy Davis Jr., Frank Sinatra and Johnny Cash have graced Vegas. The tradition of well-known artists continues today with Drake, Lady Gaga,Selena Gomez, Gwen Stefani, Britany Spears, Lionel Richie, Diana Ross and Celine Dion. DJs like Zedd and Calvin Harris have found their place with pool parties and all-night EDM clubs, keeping the Vegas heartbeat going. Vegas never sleeps, like me when I had a college paper due. How many places are 24/7 in the world? Vegas is also always reinventing itself. Constantly improving and growing, like we also should be doing, trying to move forward and not looking back, unless it is something to learn and grow from. These concepts and genius ideas are seen in the development of Vegas and are something we can all learn from. It is a unique and effective, ever changing Vegas business model. This oasis in the desert leads the way in Sales, Marketing, Branding, Public Relations (PR) and Merchandising. The approach is done with excellence with a top-notch business and entertainment approach. There may be aspects about Las Vegas that you do not agree with, but we see in life there is always a good and the counterpart. The decisions and choices are always up to the individual. This also applies to business and personal aspirations. No one with tell you, "You have to take this job and work for me". Remember that interviewing is not a one-way street, you should also be seeing if the job is a good fit for you. Even the Las Vegas Strip is a two-way street. It is not like Hotel California, where "you can check in anytime you like, but you can never leave". A classic song from the Eagles.

One thing is for certain no one can deny the success that Vegas has in the business world and it did not happen by accident. It is always in a flex of being current, providing the best of the best. It is the picture of progress and innovation. We can apply these attributes to our own lives in being the best we can be. We all know our possibilities, but sometimes we get in our own way. The Las Vegas Strip is lined with a movie set look, that displays 24/7 Lights, Camera and Action. I have always heard the phrase "What's in a name". When I say "Vegas", I believe we all would have words or a series of visuals, that would represent this place. Let's have fun with it and list what comes to mind, take a moment to make your list. To me Las Vegas is, top-notch fun, entertainment that never stops, being ultra-relaxed, too many options, international appeal, oasis in the desert, crowds, activity, endless shopping and desires. Now think about it in terms of business and then focus on how it can apply to you. This is what comes to mind for me: Activity, Productivity, Action, conventions, negotiation, and an International Global business market. Now think of you and how the concept of Vegas pertains to you. It could include Opportunity, conventions/meetings, where business happens. One stop shop, branding, marketing, selling yourself (from a business perspective) even that does not sound right, you know what I mean, lol. The list continues with success, luxury, risk-taking, investment, social, networking, reinventing yourself, the best of the best (Chefs, restaurants, hotels and entertainment), effort, passion, going all out, making money (losing money-risk taking) or attempting to and entertainment. What from the list motivates you and there is no wrong answer? Words applied like effort and passion, can go a long way! One example is stepping out of your comfort zone and taking challenges and risks. When you sit down at the blackjack table at the Venetian, there is elements of risk. Sometimes it is an important move to make a change and show the cards you have been dealt. I have learned this firsthand. I stayed with an IT company, because I liked my position, while colleges around me were making job changes and expanding their careers with new opportunities. I ultimately got laid off, after years of dedication. Inside I was thinking how loyal I was to this company. There were thousands laid off nationwide, so it was not personal. I had come up with a phrase that I tell myself all the time "risk equals benefit". Not only gambling but investing in the stock market can be risky but can also bring monetary rewards. I like to go a little deeper, believe in yourself, step out and be vulnerable, yes that is a risk but, it could have life changing results, it did for me. We are now ready to dive into the amazing pool at the Venetian, who is the dj today. Our trip to Vegas has just begun, let's make the most of our adventure together!

3

Your Vegas Guide "Phono"

This book or shall I say saga, is in part my personal journey on finding jobs, a career and finding myself along the way. I have been lost in the desert of life trying to find the lights of Vegas. It does not help me to be terrible with directions.

I am one of those late bloomers and I am still blooming. It is not easy to bloom in the desert. I have always heard go for your Plan A and if that does not work out than follow up with Plan B. I told one of my brothers (I have four brothers). I have done Plan A and B and now I am working my way through the alphabet Plan- LMNOP, I am not sure what letter, I am on now. I have also been through many LMAO Plans. I think that phase can help also, sometimes you do have to laugh at those times, it can all be an artificial process. Just so you know I am very silly and goofy, and I will never grow up, growing up is overrated, "but what do I know", maybe I will try it sometime. I wrote a song called **"Sometimes you Got to Laugh"** during a difficult time in my life. The chorus goes **"Sometime you got to laugh instead of crying, sometimes you got to give and keep on trying, life can be so hard, there is no denying, Sometimes you got to laugh, instead of crying"** I have lived these words. Giving to someone else can get your eyes off yourself and it can be life changing for the many people, you can help.

In this book I speak about my **"Trial and Errors"** and the Triumphs. I grew up in Newport Beach, CA a wealthy community in the OC.

The kids around me drove Porsche's, BMW etc. Not in our house, our limo, was the burgundy color station wagon. My dad and mom kept us grounded, we did not live like that. I was smaller, then the kids I grew up with and I found solace in my own world. I loved the idea of "Love" and all I wanted was romance, the Prince and Princess story. I was bullied throughout my elementary and Jr. High school days; my last name is Waters and I was called "Little Drip" or "Little WaWa" later and more recent "Gimpy" you will learn why later our journey together. Recently people that have been listening to my music from all over the world many are calling me "Phono". This is because my band is called "Phonoville" and currently I am the only one in the band. I find this interesting, the word "phono" in the Greek means a voice, a sound. Later in this book you will find the significance of this meaning to me. My dad would always say "what's in a word", now it makes sense. When coming up with the name of the band. I never thought deeply about the name, it just came to me. It now has a deeper meaning. I stayed back my 6th grade year because I did not mature enough physically to go to Jr. High, it was my choice. It was suggested by the school principle and my teacher. It was a good choice. We will go into more detail later. I had long hair when those around me were short haired and preppy. I was not a rebel at all, I was gentle, fun, a peace maker, a fixer, and the teachers would comment on my big brown eyes. They were big because I was very curious about this thing called life and they were wide open for the adventures that were ahead of me.

I am one of four brothers and second to the oldest. As far as back as I can remember my passion was for music and it is still there. My first band was in 6th grade. One advantage of having brothers, was when they got tired of something it was fair game. My oldest brother had a guitar and stopped playing it, so I picked it up. The band needed a bass player, so I removed two strings on the Supertone guitar, and a bass was created. The guitar was one of my favorite colors aqua blue. During this time, I also played saxophone in the school band. I was terrible at the saxophone, but there was a reason. Growing up can be difficult and Trying to understand yourself can be challenging, at least it was for me. You may be saying, what does this have to do with **"How To Get a Job Vegas Style"**, it has everything to do with this title and statement. As mentioned before my career has been all about "Trial and Error" and mainly Error, but Triumphs also happened. I use the term "Error" and it is a harsh word, but I do not see it as a word to avoid. In every career or job, there are times you can see error transform into triumph. It is the same with the word "trials", they can help us to learn new pathways to triumphs. We will go into more detail later. I am passionate about learning and striving to be better at everything in my life, so I stay in **"Learn Mode"**.

Now back to my passion music. I was very slender and small, and I looked younger than I was. I really did not fit in anywhere. I loved the ocean and many early mornings and after school, I would ride my skateboard and or cycle down to the beach to body board. Back then I was made fun of because I did not use a surfboard. I would have been a surfer, but I was so small I could carry the surfboard and a body board was much easier. I hung out at 40th street in Newport Beach, CA because it was always had the "black ball" flag, a term meaning no surfboards or hard boards allowed. This was a good thing because I had experiences when a surfer was upset, because I supposedly took their wave. Next, they would airborne their surfboard and launch it at me, hitting me at various places in body. I never fitted in, I was not in the surfer click or any other click, I was in my own world. I am an extrovert not at all an introvert, but I felt very isolated in the world. I have always been in bands, the drummer in my first band, grew weed in his closet and smoked it, as well as the members. For myself I never tried it growing up or drinking alcohol, but I accepted everyone, I am not judgmental. I had one best friend and if we were not in the ocean, we were writing songs with our band called Destiny, we shared a love for the Beatles and the music of KISS, this was my second band. Yes, we dressed up like them. I was the "Star Child" and he was the "Demon". I found out not only was I slow growing up physically, but I also had a learning disability, I have or had a high IQ, but I am also dyslexic, now there is a confusing mind game. When I was young, I was never told the term, it was taboo then to talk about then. All I know is that I went to a special after-school program, in the evening taught by nuns. In high school I played water polo because my older brother played. My first day of school and practice, I was thrown into the water with my backpack on and all my new schoolbooks and supplies. I heard "How is the temperature, Waters"? I also will not forget one time, three guys on the team, grabbed and threw me into the deep end of the Olympic size pool. They brought me to the bottom 12 feet down of the pool and the three held me down. I was at their mercy as I looked up. I thought I really was going to drown. Later I found out, they had been drinking and taking many shots of tequila. Throughout high school, I felt like I was in an old school pinball game, getting knocked around and landing in the holes of life and sometimes missing all the holes and landing between the paddles. My life at times also felt like bowling alley, when the pins are swept away, and you must start new again. I did well in soccer and baseball and loved both sports, but I played water polo, go figure. It all made sense later, when I transferred to another school in Irvine, CA and I met one of my best friends. My friend and I shared a love for music, and he played the drums, so we had a band together, soon I met another lifetime friend. The High School I was at before was called Newport Harbor and our coaches, were also the Olympic coaches. This school was known for its Water polo. When the coach at University High School in Irvine heard I was coming there, the whole team was excited. They did not realize, I was the worst player on the Newport Beach team history, this was not debatable it was a fact! I really was a letdown and I felt it. I will never forget, there was a big rival water polo event in Long Beach, CA. Newport Harbor High School against University High School. I was beyond nervous. I remember we all were lined up on our designated sides of the pool. I heard echoes of voices across the pool saying, "I get Waters", "no I get Waters", "Waters, you traitor", "Little WaWa, your all wet, you're done". Oh Sh...t! Have you ever seen when a frenzy of sharks is attacking something? All the splashing and insanity taking place, well that was about to be the scene. This is another tattooed memory. What I learned, is we all can get off the path, but it does not mean, we are too far away from it, to get back on it. Now regarding academics, I always struggled with anything math and still do, but I excelled in English. It is funny in Jr. college I decided to minor is music. I play by ear and write music this way. I learned that music theory is very mathematical and advanced music theory was the only "F" I have ever received. After Orange Coast College, I attended UCLA and was excepted as an English major. I was shocked I got accepted into the program, it was a difficult school to get into. My goal was to work in the music business and while at UCLA I interned at A & M records, part of the large Universal Music Group family. UCLA did not have a music business degree, so I also enrolled in the certificate in the Music Business program at UCLA Extension. For me college I really majored in "Trial and Error". I have learned a lot from the school called **Trial and Error University (T&EU)** or in some cases the **University of (TMI)** To Much Information and I have received honoree degrees from both. I should have my masters there soon. I struggled throughout all my college experience and joining a fraternity may not have been the best decision. That just touches of the surface of who I am. I will go into more throughout this book.

4

The Surface Of Planet "Vegas"

We have also just explored the surface of Vegas, we have now landed here on this unique planet, let us take a moment and decompress. Las Vegas sits between California and Arizona. To me whenever I fly into the Phoenix airport, I always feel like I am landing on Mars. I look at all the red rock mountains and it reminds me of the red planet. With one company I worked for, I traveled there once a month for seven years. Now what planet does California remind me, this I do not have an answer. They call Los Angeles, City of the Angles, but I thought that was in Anaheim. My Dodger fan friends, will not like this comment. I am just playing, but I am an Anaheim Angels fan, when most of my friend's root for the Dodgers. It is all about choices. One choice is where you fit in for a career, how to uncover your interests and apply them to a job and hopefully it leads to a career. When you are in Vegas and you see the Eiffel Tower at Paris, Paris you know it is not the actual Eiffel Tower, but an amazing replica. If you think it was imported there from Paris, Houston we have a problem, it is time for a History 101 course or New York New York was taken from New York and the Vegas tram is the actual New York subway. But seriously, the process of interviewing is like that similarity. The process of being interviewed, however it is just a thumb sketch of who you are, as it pertains to work. It is an artificial sweetener, not the sugar of who you are. You have on your suit on covering your partially wrinkled dress shirt. You come prepared with the highlights of your work experience. It is just a rough sketch, the Cliff notes to your time at the job before or internships. So right from the start you are a summary, just trying to present the highlights of who you are and what you have done. Instead of "Speed Dating" you are **"Speed Interviewing"**. The Interviewer does not know you and you do not know them, try, and remember this thought. Before the yes arrives, there may be no's, try not to take it personally. Have a bit of fun with this **"awkward dance"**, this is what I call the interview process. This is your rehearsal to the "Play" of your life and if you want to be more creative and add music the **"Musical"** of your life. Can you imagine doing a song and dance of your resume, like a Vegas production. Early in my career my opening song would be "My Resume Sucks"! I would sing my anthem with all my heart, as I would walk out of the interview doors. I did not hear applause's, as I exited the building, more like silence. I remember being interviewed for an IT company in Austin, Texas. I had to have three in person interviews in one day for this job. I interviewed with three of the owners for this software company and they all were going well. In my last interview, we were speaking about sports. Now I am not an expert on the subject, and I mentioned my brother went to OU in Oklahoma. I could not have said anything worse, there is a huge rivalry between the Texas Longhorns and the OU Sooners. If you live in any of these and surrounding states, you will know exactly what I am saying. As I made my comment, I then saw on the wall he went to UT. The interviews were going very well, until then. He became visibly upset and the interview ended, and I was told "we will get back to you". He made some comments about his dislike for OU and his nonverbal responses spoke volumes and I never heard from them again. What I leaned being in **"Learn Mode"**, is you are entering their world, it is by their rules, it is their environment, you are a guest. We may not like this structure, but it is a reality, to play by their rules, if you are interested in the job. All sports games have rules of engagement and the "corporate sport" has its rules of their game. If you want to play ball with them, know their rules, do the company research, and read the reviews from current teammates there. Do I really look at it as a game, I really do and we need to understand this game very well, to become a "First String" player! Vegas is a game as well! All the lights and the movie set look of the hotels are designed to lure you into the casino, for what purpose, to play games, slot machines, sit down at the blackjack table and spend money. All though this can conjure up a negative thought, it can also be a positive one. When comparing preparing for a sport, you must practice, prepare, strategic preparation, and know your competition. The same in the interview process, the same principles apply, and it should all be done with excellence. I have heard many say over the years, "I am a natural" and that can be true. Some also think they can wing it for an interview. The one thing they forget, is there is a lot of people that are competing for the same job and many of them also have "natural talent". Do not fool yourself, develop your natural talent and be better, we all can grow and improve, this should never stop.

5

Vegas Is Always Open And Changing

One thing is for certain no one can deny the success that Vegas has in the business world and it did not happen by accident. It is always in a flex of being current, providing the best of the best. It is the picture of progress and innovation. It never stops improving and being better! The Las Vegas Strip lined with the movie set look, that displays a 24/7 of Lights, Camera, Action, and it is always open for business. One example of this is the Bellagio it has beautiful water fountains and a water show that is synced with music and inside the hotel high-end designer shops. I remember once in front of the Bellagio; I had a new iPhone and I was videoing the water show and my iPhone fell out of my hands and cracked on some stones and fell into the water. You can only imagine how horrible the video on playback looked with the major cracked screen and water drenched phone. Can you also imagine the words that came out of my mouth in sync with the music! You may at times have felt rained on and cracked and in need of repair, I sure have. But like the old relics of "Old Vegas" downtown, that looks like a scene from old Rome. We can be restored and reinvent ourselves like we see demonstrated in real time in Las Vegas. This is happening everyday in Las Vegas, renovation and repair.

What we see, hear, know, and experience in Vegas can be brought to life and applied on a personal and career level. Vegas is always rebuilding and improving, in the same way we all should be bettering ourselves in growing our career and our character.

My hope is you see the business traits of Vegas you will see how it can apply to you. (My approach to this book is in chill mode, so you could be reading this on a trip to Las Vegas, by the pool at the Venetian or snowed in somewhere dreaming about Vegas. The process of writing this book has been very enjoyable. Maybe we all can meet someday in Vegas and share our successes).

My dad always told me "why do people have many clocks in their homes, it is just a reminder that time is running out" there is truth to that statement. Unfortunately, my dad passed away at a young age in his early 60's. My dad was a road scholar, very funny and a loving dad. I had the privilege to work with some startup companies with him, we also coached soccer "Futbol" together and had many walks at night through the hills of Irvine, CA, because he was frustrated with the lack of direction of my life, while I was in high school. My dad was very accomplished he was a Patent Attorney and earlier in his career a physiologist. He worked directly with Neil Armstrong, Buzz Aldrin and the other astronauts from the Apollo space programs and space shuttle. My first career choice after music was to be an astronaut. My four brothers and I grew up around space food and space suits, can you imagine how cool it was when my dad was brought into our classes space stuff for show and tell. If you look at my record covers for my band "Phonoville" some are space themed. On the first record on the rocket is "W7", this stands for my family which is seven of us, five brothers and my mom and dad. My dad is the captain of the Phonoville rocket. Now he is conducting flights in the Heavens!

6

The Lights Of Vegas

When you sit down at the blackjack table at the Aria, there is elements of risk. Sometimes it is an important move to make a change and show the cards you have been dealt. As I mentioned I came up with a phrase that I tell myself all the time **"Risk Equals Benefit"**. I like to go a little deeper, believe in yourself, step out and be vulnerable, yes that is a risk but, it could have life changing results, it did for me. As you know by now music has always been and will always be my passion. I got married in my early 20's to a girl from Australia. She had been living in London when we met and began to date. We were to move to London and my music was pop with a very European sound. This was my Plan A, there was no Plan B. My ex-wife was not only a model but was doing well in the apparel industry. Music and apparel are very compatible industries, I think. We had our plan, after snow skiing in the local mountains in Southern California for our honeymoon, a quick trip to Vegas, to gamble our life savings (I had to add Vegas to this story, that part did not happen). So, to the ski slopes we went, my ex-wife could not ski, so she had coffee in the resort, while I ventured the slopes. I am a reckless skier not purposely; it comes naturally to me. This ski trip, I never fell, which is a miracle. I was in the process of having a record deal, from someone extremely high up in the music industry, he had signed large artists at the time. Somewhere on the mountain I began to have pain in my right leg, severe shooting pain up and down my leg. I thought to myself, I have not fallen yet, why the pain and why is the pain so extreme. The pain never went away but continued. There is so much more to this story, but I will leave that for another book I am writing. When we got back to Newport Beach, California, I went immediately to the Doctor. I was there for many hours and had many x-rays. The Doctor said go to Cedars Sinai in Los Angeles or Scripps Clinic in San Diego. I had my parents in San Diego, so we chose that location. This is when the nightmare began. After days of tests, MRI's, Bone Scans, CT scans, blood work, I went back to my parents and we waited for results. I will never forget when the Doctor called, my mom answered phone and she handed it to me. "Hi Brian this your Doctor from Scripps Clinic, I have bad news to tell you, you have Osteosarcoma, a pediatric bone cancer, we believe it is very advanced and your odds of survival are not good, the cancer cells are very aggressive and we believe it has metastasized from your femur bone and also to your lungs" I then dropped the phone tears fell in the silent room, just like they are for me now, as I relive that moment. I also dropped my dreams, with the phone. Life can be unexpected. This is my journey on rebuilding the dream and finding hope again. The streets of Las Vegas are full of broken dreams. Living in California especially Los Angeles are people, our friends trying to find their dreams in the movies, television, theater, and music. You can sense the excitement, but also the desperation and depression. The streets of these cities are displaying the real-life drama, of the reality of their struggles. We all have dreams and we all have stories, never give up on hope and try not to lose yourself or compromise your soul on a fix of a dream. Dreams are awesome but sometimes we have the nightmare ones and mine was about to begin, chemotherapy, having to make major decisions that I felt I was unable and not equipped to make. One decision was with my right leg itself. The Oncologists wanted me to amputate the leg at the hip- right away, because the tumor was so large it was ready to break out of my femur, it was larger than a lemon. At the same time, a world-renowned Doctor had been involved with my case, he was only one of two Doctors that knew a new procedure called limb salvage, allograft surgery. Basically, they remove a large portion of the femur and do a bone transplant, with a cadaver bone. Now picture me in my early 20's hearing all this for the first time. Someone else's bone in my body and major screws and stainless-steel plates, that will stay in my leg, I would be bionic. The scary part was that I also had to do pre-chemo before the surgery could happen. The tumor would remain in my body for several months. Sarcomas spread fast and the Doctors were worried about possible tumor cells in my lungs already, this is where I also applied **"Risk Equals Benefit"** a very simple three words, with ever changing life decisions. What if the chemotherapy does not work? Just remove the leg completely and the tumor will be out of your body? I believe in God and I saw firsthand with this experience many times His intervention and His guiding hand throughout this experience. My Mom and dad were a huge support system as well as family. You may ask, how did I make this decision. My orthopedic surgeon said to me. "I will treat you like my brother" "I will do it for free, If I have to" "Trust me". I said "Let's do this" , yes now here as the words go to paper more tears are falling from my eyes and I am asking you **"Let's do this"** , I am here and I believe in everyone reading this book, has gifts and talents, yet to be discovered or developed more. Many know their path, mine was always music. What I learned is to have the focus of an eagle and the work ethic and tenacity of a pigeon. I have always felt bad for the pigeon, they are not a loved bird, I have never heard of anyone with a pet pigeon. First, have you ever noticed their heads are always bobbing. Wouldn't this make their world view blurry and looking at the blurry lights on the streets of Vegas dizzying. Yet I would say they are the busiest birds I have ever encountered. They never give up, they are persistent, resilient, and basically do not give a damn. They are bullied by the crows, by people and they keep coming back to this boxing ring of life. Do they ever think, I wish I were a parrot? I would say not, they are more interested in the In N Out Burger and fries you are eating, yes there are in Las Vegas, but why are there not any slot machines in their locations there? Nothing gets the pigeon down; they hear all day long "get out of here" and they come right back. We can learn a lot from the pigeon, don't give up! This has been a journey and thought process of mine, so let us all be a kinder to the pigeon and I proclaim a day in honor of our very resourceful feathered friend. Don't get me started about a year ago I had another friend, I called him Fred. This was in Clearwater, FL. He was a cockroach that was missing a leg, so it was hard for him to get around. I felt compassion for him because as I mentioned I came very close to having one of my legs amputated. This is another resourceful insect, that I would say is more hated than the pigeon. I would put out a little food and water in the kitchen. Every night we would meet there, really. He was not scared; he would struggle across the floor to get to the food. My entire time in that apartment that was our routine. Now the mosquito is like the people that are toxic and trying derail your life or dreams, you know what I am talking about and I am sure a few names pop up in your head right away. The only credit I will give the mosquito, is they warn you before the suck your blood and leave a nice red itchy sore bump on you. I wrote a comedy skit on them. I thought how funny the mosquitoes must be in Colorado or California where weed (Marijuana) is legal. I picture someone smoking some weed and the vampire insect comes flying over sucks the blood and is high saying "Yo Bro" lets chill, I am super hungry". When I was going through high dose chemotherapy my whole body would be toxic, with basically poison and I would put out welcome signs to the mosquitoes "Come taste my blood" and I am sure they would not be happy afterwards. How does this relate to Vegas, well they all are at the summer homes, resorts and yes you will find them on the golf courses as well. Everything I mention and the creatures we share earth with on earth all have a common consistency, persistence, and a great work ethic. Does the ant say, "can I take my two-week vacation'? I am not going to answer that because I do not know, but I think based on my conversations with my ant friend Mary, the answer is 'no' (this I am kidding, but Henry the cockroach is true).

    I have been to Vegas many times for fun, but most has been work related for sales events with companies I have worked for. I represented in

Vegas companies like Hewlett Packard (hp) and many other large corporations. Take a moment and jot down a quick list, just write out, what interests you in a business. What would you like to do day to day at a job/career? (We will get back to that list) later. When deciding on a job or career, also try the Pro's and Con's list and when making the list be honest with yourself. I remember one time I was doing this exercise and I thought, wow there are a lot of cons, I better add some more Pro's, if that is the case, start over.

Have you ever flown into Vegas at night, at first sight, the area is completely dark! In the distance one starts to see, a glimpse of color, the lights begin to become brighter and brighter, you can feel the anticipation as you approach it closer and then there, she, is the Oasis in the desert. Your senses come alive you can almost hear the slot machines, smell the smoke, and see the sights. (as mentioned before, there is always turbulence when you fly into Vegas) and to continue that note, when looking for a job/Career there is going to be turbulence, guaranteed! But you will also land! When you step out on the Strip in Vegas, you are presented with choices. What are you going to do with your time? Where are you going to spend your time and what is it going to take to get you there? This question can apply also when trying to figure out the direction of your career. We spend at least 8 hours a day in a job or career. I purposely draw a distinction between the two, hopefully we all end up in a career. Many times, a job can direct us to the career. We all would like a career. We all want purpose and passion, Vegas has all that and it never sleeps, open all night. Some people may gravitate to non-profit work.

Giving to someone else can get your eyes off yourself and it can be life changing for many people. Many people find fulfillment in this kind of work and the world sure needs the help! One step is mindset.

I think of Nike, they understand this step. Don't just state a plan, as Nike says, "Just Do It". They have made that statement for many years and it still applies.

The business climate today is a speed boat, in the past it was more of a cruise ship, you got on the corporate ship and you stayed on. If I lived in that era, I would have written the book "How to Get a Job Cruise Style." I would have worn a polyester, bell bottom suit as well. After deep consideration, I would not have worn the suit, unless it was a space suit!

As mentioned before, I have always thought the interview process to get a job was "artificial" it is the sweeteners not the real sugar of who you are. They say if your given lemons make lemonade, but they also forget to say add sugar. The sugar of you is your gifts and talents, it is what makes you, you. This is also true with the company and what they can offer you. My thought continues, if you could master the art of writing a great resume and get down the art of interviewing, that alone could land you a job. A candidate could fool a company I figure for about six-months to a year, then move on to the next company. Of course, I am being vicious. When you read employment hiring documents, companies today are "at will", they can fire you or let you go for any reason. If you are in sales, usually there is a 90-day period to prove your selling aptitude.

I have had to reinvent myself many times and change the direction of the course I was on. I had dreams and job aspirations and have wandered many years in the desert never seeing the lights of Vegas, I was in the dark. Stars do not always align, and the road traveled can be full of disappointment, that is reality. The other reality in Las Vegas is the Oasis in the desert, innovative and very resourceful. These are characteristics we should model.

When I was growing up, I the idea that anything is possible and that dreams can come true, follow your heart. There is nothing wrong with that thought process if you live in a bubble. I do not want to sound negative, but one part left out is we live in a world of chaos, everyone around has the same dream you do, now talk about a mind game. Even if some get to their destination or accomplish the goals they set, the result, can sometimes leave them empty and unfulfilled. The search for fulfillment cycle continues. I knew a wealthy family where I grew up in Newport Beach. I lived in the area where movie star legends and sports celebrities lived. The father was a pro baseball scout. His son's dream was to play baseball and his whole life was directed that way. After years of dedication and sacrifices, he became first string pitcher for the Oakland A's, his dream came true. In his first season he had what is called "Tommy Johns" an injury to his arm and his career was over in a moment. I heard from families that knew him, that he experienced years of depression and sadness. He was lost, his dreams were shattered, for many years I heard he just gave up. Then he became a church pastor and he found purpose and fulfillment again. My suggestion is be focused with a purpose, but like a retro pinball machine, there are many slots the ball can go into, it may not get you a 100 points, but you might score 85 points, which is better than 0. I can relate to his story and I would guess, many readings this has experienced a career loss or personal loss. My mom always says, "life is a process of letting go", this is true, we had to say goodbye to my dad when he passed away from colon cancer. My dad was so gifted a road scholar. My dad had the most giving heart, humorous, but he passed away with so many dreams he had yet to fulfill. One of my brothers always says "bloom where you are planted" these are great statements, and both have a lot of depth and truth. Strive to have no regrets, I say it this way because I have had regrets and regrets will leave you on the side of the lonely desert road to Vegas. Words like "I wish I", "If Only I", now there is only ("Me, Myself and I). As you know, I try now not to take life to seriously. Yes, there is a time and place for that and I prefer an open hand to a closed fist. You cannot change the past, but you can learn and get off the repeat patterns, I wrote a song called **"Walk in the Light"** here is some of the words. **"The roller-coaster life you can't get off, you're up and your down, you're in then you're out"**. Another song I wrote is called **"Can't Rewind"**. There are many times in life, I would like to redo or a least get a refund for the time lost, I also have a song soon to be released called **"Lost Time"** "got to keep moving, I am tired of loosing, got to make up for Lost Time". When I write songs, to me they are my journals, my thoughts. Like the tide of the ocean, it comes in and it goes out.

I had my dream, a simple dream. Here goes, get a band together, write songs and perform for a living. As you know by now, I have always loved music, I still remember songs I wrote in 6th grade. In that the same year I started to learn saxophone, attempted is more like it. I would drive my family crazy. We had a two-story house in Newport Beach, California. I used to go in the stair well area and blast sounds with my saxophone. I would hit notes, that were unbearable, even our dog would run for cover. The reverb acoustics were awesome to me, my family had a different opinion. Music is my passion and always has been. Throughout High School, I continued to play in bands. We would practice for hours in our drummer's family garage in Irvine. We would start early on a Saturday morning and go all day. We played loud in Irvine is in the hills of Orange County, CA. A few years ago, I ran into a girl that went to our high school and lived in Irvine. She said that every weekend there was this band and they were so loud, and we would drive around, trying to find out where the sound was coming from, to make it stop. Because of the canyon and hills our sound just echoed everywhere and we were stealth, no one could pinpoint what garage we were playing in. There was no doubt we were dedicated musicians and because of the hours of practicing, we also did improve. My Junior year I began to play with a known alternative Christian band in Southern California, I was the youngest member in the band, the other players were in their late 20's at the time. This led to a band I started called the "Proclaimers" which included two close friends and we played for several years live and some of the crowds we would play for would be in the thousands. I could go into more detail on that journey later, but I need to stay focused, which is a challenge for me. After high school, I went to Orange Coast College and studied marketing and music, which included music theory. Earlier I mention that I failed music theory, but I write music. I play by ear, as many well-known artists do in the music industry. I mention this because like Vegas, you may arrive, but the next important step is where you fit in. For example, you may find a job in a large corporation that you love, but you could end up in the wrong department. Unless you have a plan to direct yourself into a division that would utilize your skills, you could get stuck. This happened to me with the company PepsiCo, they were owners of Pepsi and at the time KFC, Pizza Hut and Taco bell restaurants. I was in the legal department and I wanted to be in marketing, it never happened. It was as if I was trapped in the legal department, where my skills were not being utilized. I was accepted after Orange Coast College to UC Santa Barbara and UCLA. I chose UCLA because it was in the heart of the music industry. It was tough because I also loved the ocean and body boarding, Santa Barbara would have been great for that. Body Boarding professionally was my plan B, if you believe that, well just do not believe that.

I joined a fraternity, because they said they did not haze, you were not a pledge but an associate member. I received the nickname "Gumby" and it was all downhill from there. That story would take a novel to explain. I got into UCLA as an English major and I left UCLA, with some music industry experience, but without a degree. I was physically exhausted, and I overall just did not feel well. I remember I called my dad and said I got to get out of here. I was living in the fraternity house; it was not a healthy environment. I left one day, when the frat house was empty. I told no one and I never looked back. Maybe some have had a great experience with the fraternal system, but for me my first quarter I was on academic probation and got alcohol poisoning. This was not going to end well for "Gumby". Today I have no friends from the fraternity, the day I left was the day those friendships ended. I did learn what true friendship is and what it is not. Good friendships encourage and build you up, not tear you down. My best friends from high school are still my friend close friends today. One of my friends drove me home from UCLA many weekends and would pull over to the side of the freeway so I could throw up, because my friends in the Fraternity wanted to see "Gumby" get drunk. I do not blame the brothers in the fraternity, it was always my choice, expect possibly the initiation rush time. Have a great college experience, but we wise. My house every year would have parties near Las Vegas on house boats. Years before I was there, I heard of what happened on a fraternity trip. A drunk brother of the house fell into the water and no one could find him. Then his friend who was drunk also dove in to try and find him, they both never came to the surface. I never did attend that trip or any of those kinds of trips. They were always a possible recipe for disaster.

After UCLA I ended up working several retail jobs, without a degree it was hard to take it to the next level. We will go later in the book with the chapter **"To Degree or not Degree, that is the Question"**. Now back to you, look at yourself and come up with positive statements. Choose words like dedicated, hardworking, creative, caring, positive, words that pertain to you. Everyone has something positive, search for you and be honest. All of these are desirable attributes that a company would look for. My job path has been very reactive in the past, notice job and not saying career. The career aspect has evolved later in my work experience. Have your career direction but don't stay in auto pilot, know when to stay in a job and when to leave. Always try and leave on a good note. Your resume is the pathway to where you will settle in your career. It is the road map to where you have been or going in your career direction. Let us just say, I have taken the scenic route and not always by choice. As I mentioned this book is in part the "Trial and Errors" of my work experiences. On another note I have had many amazing career experiences and these I will also share.

Another work experience I had was with a major hotel in Newport Beach, CA. My youngest brother also worked there, his job position at the hotel was the pool lifeguard. My job was the "Greeter" I.E the "Clown". He wore a swimsuit and I wore a suit also. Let me describe it. It was peach/coral suit jacket in color with matching pants, but really moving toward pink, included in my fashion presentation a purple shirt and a floral tie. I would greet the guests, get their luggage, and get them to their rooms. In addition to also being a comic relief (This was done, just by guests looking at what I was wearing), my job also included escorting guests in a hotel van to destinations along the Newport Beach coastline and trips to the airports. I made some good tips; hindsight I believe they were sympathy tips. So, one day I got to work, and I forgot the floral tie, major panic my outfit was not complete. I got in the hotel van and rushed home to get it. At the time, I lived with my parents on Balboa Island, definitely a great location on the Balboa bay yes where the OC was filmed. One problem was the streets were narrow. Now I did not see it at the time, but there was a large new monster truck parked on my street and it had extended mirrors protruding from the vehicle, yes it was a transformer style truck. As I passed by my van ran into the beautiful chrome extended mirror and the metal mirror folded and became one with car, it was not a pretty sight. This is what followed. A guy who was beyond furious came out to his truck and observed the damage I caused. Yelling words in anger F.....k Y....u, yes, every word that are not in the standard dictionary, wow he was mad. I slowly started to open my van door and come out and face the music. I felt like I was in a western and this was the showdown and I knew I would lose on the draw. I came out the van and he was in the process to take a swing at me. But once he saw me in my floral suit, he had a complete compassion reaction. The power of the suit and all its colors caused him to be frozen in his tracks. He had instant pity on me and all he said was "God bless you' he got in his truck and drove away. Conclusion he thought I was in worse shape than his truck. To be forced to wear the suit. I had it bad. Sometimes we must pay our dues, to get to our goals. I see it all the time in Las Vegas, people working two jobs, to get to their dreams. Like a vehicle, goals are the fuel that gets us there. Try and see the good in your current situations. Like the bad having to wear the suit, I found the good, in making people happy showing them around the beautiful beaches in Southern California. Find the places that are free, for me the go to place is the beach. We should follow that example. Every wave that comes to shore is unique. Every sunset is unique. Every person in this world is unique. This means you! You can make an impact in this world because I believe everyone has a gift or talent to express. Unfortunately, some never find the key to start their engine. What I have learned is be careful seeking affirmation or direction from other people. Everyone has an opinion, but no one is you or knows you better than you. I used to seek everyone's approval and try to live up to some unidentified expectation, the conclusion was always failure. You know in your heart your passions. I would add, if it is a healthy direction for you, then you do not need endorsement from other people. The reason is some people operate out of fear or just want to settle, let that be there path and determine your own way. We all will have crossroads and we will all have to make choices. I have another quote that came to me during my time in the hospital. It could be interpreted as depressing or how I see it as a motivator, I would not call it inspiring, however. This came to me on the eleventh floor the cancer floor, where I basically lived for a few years. "We come into the world crying and screaming, hopefully we don't leave that way". I saw some who left this world in peace and some who left crying and screaming on the cancer floor. We come into the world alone and leave alone, you are responsible for your own actions, try and make good choices. I wrote a song called the **"Eleventh Floor"** about my experience on the cancer floor of the hospital in San Diego. Being newly married , it was beyond difficult going through cancer treatments. I could write a novel about our relationship, really a series of novels, but I will try and stay focused. We dated and got married after a year and a half. We were financially struggling; she was not able to work her country her Visa ran out and my visa credit card was maxed out. So she lived with my parents until we got married. When my chemo treatments started, we both moved in with my parents. What a blessing that they opened their home so warmly to us. My parents also make sacrifices for our brothers.

    I was happy about getting married but concerned how would I be able to provide a good job and take care of my new bride, so many unknowns. The decision was made in large because she had to leave the

HOW TO GET A JOB VEGAS STYLE

country. I did not want that to happen, so we married. Our goal as mentioned before was in the future to live in London and I would work in music with my record deal and she in apparel. We had not started opening our wedding gifts, when I got the news about my bone cancer. I was from my experience forever changed. In some ways for the good, but I also became very fearful, what if it comes back. during my chemotherapy, my blood count would become very low and I would be very vulnerable to getting sick, because the treatments effected my immune system. For several years after my treatments, I became a germophobe. This was going to be my second band name choice, if I did not choose Phonoville. I am completely kidding. everywhere I went I was careful about touching door knobs etc. I got through it. One of the chemotherapy drugs, I had because of the doses I had, my heart had to be monitored for five years. The concern was my heart could enlarge during that time, from the prolonged side effects of the drug. I also lived in fear for those years to be honest. Any tightness in the chest or pain, would trigger "what was that " reaction inside me.

Today I have my leg; I am very blessed, during my treatments and for years after I walked with crutches and then to a cane. I had many years of adjustments and frustrations. I lost a lot of range of motion in my leg. I used to run and play water polo and lived in the ocean, those days are gone. Being young in my 20's I grew up real fast. I found out during and after who my true friends were and that this world and the people in it can be kind and very cruel. My ex-wife also said at the I feel like we have been married for forty years and not it was not a positive comment, after being married less than a year. There is a word called momentum, when you are in it, you know it and when it stops, it is like hitting a wall. I was naive when I finished almost two years of chemotherapy. I thought people would help and I would be able to pick up where I left off with a great career. Surprise! Now here we go on my job/career search adventure, we have officially arrived at our destination Las Vegas.

7

The Action Of Vegas

I like many of you have grow up with dreams, I still have dreams and goals. My dreams were well defined and focused then. I wanted to be a Singer-Songwriter since I can remember. I still have songs I wrote on the scraps of paper from elementary school, I am bit of a hoarder, but a recovering one. My dream never left as the years went on. People would try to redirect my path and focus, out of protecting me from being hurt and rejected, in the cut-throat music industry, but I was determined and dedicated. I stared playing in bands and at the time the bass was not what people gravitated toward, so I picked up the bass. My brothers and I would put on concerts for family and anyone who would listen. I played in copy bands all the way through. In high school the Proclaimers formed .We were together for years and played a lot of gigs, many had thousands attending. It came to a halt, one night sat my birthday party. We had a large group at a restaurant called the Spaghetti Factory in Newport Beach California. A guy sitting next to me did not know me and asked a question "How do you think they are going to get rid of the singer and keep the name". I turned to him and said, "I am the singer". His expression was of complete shock, let's just say a conversation followed. They always say bands are like marriages. There had been tension, the band started as a three piece and became a 5 piece. I was told to focus on vocals, by some members and to get a dedicated bass player, that happened. Then the songs I wrote, were being replaced by other songs with a different sound. I really did not care about that; it was how it was done. To sum it up, they liked the platform and the momentum of where we were as a band, but they wanted a heavier rock sound and the idea, keep the name and momentum, and get rid of me. Conclusion I pulled the plug, completely. I was devastated, betrayed, hurt, and exhausted. All of this and for what? and this is a Christian band. I think back, I should have put a new band together and finished the record and continued, but I was in shocked and lost my confidence. Really in hindsight no one in that band every regained the momentum needed in a band again.

It was not long after this period when I was diagnosed with bone cancer. I have always felt that pain is pain and it does not matter if it is physical or emotional, they both can be challenging and heartbreaking to say the least. I have been going through a breakup from a girl I love in South America, she is the most special person I have met in my life. I am experiencing pain from this very much. We all have been here and find ourselves with that lost an empty feeling. I want to help, and I want to share what I have learned. Everyone has challenges in life and what we do with them and how we handle them makes a difference. This is a journey in real time, looking for fulfillment in a job and along the way learning life lessons. My experience has been trial and error with an emphasis on error. Everyone travels a path and it leads in a certain direction. Many have clear direction on where it leads, however that route is less common. I dare to say most like myself get off track and get distracted with the scenic route. I will take it a step further I am so bad with directions in where I am going, before app navigation's, I would get lost. It became a running joke with people that know me That metaphor applies on my life journey. I hope I can encourage, motivate, and inspire the future leaders. When I looked at my life in the past, I thought I would at least have the basics down. This is how it would look. Happily married, a few children, a career and over all fulfillment, satisfied. Reality, I have two failed marriages, no children because of an ectopic pregnancy and a miscarriage and I am wondering what I am going to do when I grow up. I believe all these types of losses, they are in heaven. But you know what, I am kind of getting it now and I have found happiness in this process. In the eyes of the world I have been rich, and I have been limited on funds. I will not say poor; I have always had something for which I am very thankful. I now have a limp, when before I was very physically active, but I still can walk. You see what I have learned, even during my most bleak period during my cancer treatments I was still breathing, someone always was in a worse condition then me. I tried during that time to stay positive. My second chemo treatment was given to close to the first. It was rare how my white count was affected by the chemo and then it took a double dip and I ended up with a 0 white count and placed is a germ-free room in the hospital, that no one could enter. It was a very frightening time. I would like to say I handled well, but I was scared. I had lost a lot of weight, I heard under 100 lbs. I had a high fever; my body was basically shutting down. Then when I had my allograft surgery and assisting Doctor severed my femoral artery, this put me in intensive care, and I was not sure If I was going to be able to keep my leg. This intense of care room was like a scene from a si-fi spaceship, it could have looked that way because I was extremely high on morphine also. It was a very uncertain and scary time for me, every day was a decision to keep or remove my leg at the hip. My pulse in my leg was monitored constantly. I was inspired to get through the cancer time, to sing and write songs. When I came out of surgery I could not speak, this was caused when my leg was bleeding in surgery they went from a breathing mask to a breathing tube, in the process of panic they forced the tube down my vocal cords and they became paralyzed. After several months of not speaking they said I may not speak again. I was the guy who said he was going to write songs and sing through the chemo treatment process. At that point I was writing on a note pad and ringing a bell. There was a high chance I could lose my leg, because of the severed femur artery, but my leg was still there. Because what some would say was a mistake or error, when they examined my cancerous bone, they took out of my body, the tumor cells were all 100% dead, amazing, to me, a miracle. I was not at all in control of what was going on, but God was. Not having a voice going through chemo in the hospital was concerning. One time they were bringing some chemotherapy bag and the nurse said Mr. Randol we have your chemotherapy ready. Now I had just got my treatment the day before. I could not communicate to the nurse. I was so fortunate my ex-wife came in the room when she did and stopped the process. On the floor she got the nickname as the "bitch" by the nurses. She protected me. For all our marriage troubles I have to say she had my back then and I am grateful for that. There is so much that happened during that time, that it would take several books. The hospital was very worried about because it they knew I sang or attempted to (lol) and I had trained vocally. When I came home, there still had no improvements to my voice, only air came out. The Doctors were very concerned that I would never speak again, or my voice would be very raspy if it ever came back. I do not know the words to express the depression and despair I felt during this time. I was in extreme pain from my leg and the screws that were placed inside me. I was completely hairless and skin and bone. One person said I looked like a "friendly alien". One of my songs I write " I just can't let you see me like this, the alien that can't seem to find his ship. Strip away everything that makes me feel like you. The needle prick the IV drip as I fall into the deep abyss ".I would let know one take a picture of me during this time or the entire time of treatment. People can be very insensitive and many so-called friends, stop calling or visiting because they could not deal with it. I would think to myself, neither can I! Now I know why 90% of marriages end from this kind of situation, ours was no exception, it also ended. Today I walk and with a limp and have limited range of motion, I can't do any of those activities today or since my surgery, but I am thankful for my leg and my life. During my chemotherapy treatment and after my surgery. Where I lived was on a hill overlooking Solana Beach, the 100 steps they call, because there were many steps down to the beach. I knew this firsthand because I would go down the steps on my crutches. First, I would wrap my surgery leg in plastic saran wrap. I made my slow progress down the sandy steps to the sand. Many times, I would almost fall, if that were to happen, they would not be able to fix me. I then would hobble to the shoreline, drop my crutches, and fall into the ocean, with my body-board. It was not a graceful scene, but I did land in the water and makes a splash like the whales do. I never thought about the consequences, I just did it and many days I did it. A few weeks later, I mentioned it to my surgeon. His reaction was not positive. He said basically you have a weakened immune system from chemotherapy and an incision on your leg that goes from your knee to your hip, exposed and staples running the whole length. You then go into an ocean with millions of germs, are you insane. Let me quote a chorus from my song 11th Floor "I lost my mind a thousand times on the 11th floor, can't find my way out from these closing doors. I never asked for any of this, feels like I am always last on the waiting list". The 11th The cancer floor at UCSD hospital in San Diego, where I had lived lot of my time, home away from home. That time was a process of letting go, my lifestyle would forever changed. I had visions and dreams of running away and hiding in a cave. Many times, I wish I could just run, but I hung my running shoes up and traded them in for a walker and crutches, which were part of my life for years. I loved to ski and my honeymoon was the last time, since I got diagnosed, I hung up the skies forever. As you know during my career while I represented hp, I was called by many "gimpy". People just trying to be funny. But to me it was flashbacks to when I was bullied in school. I have had people mimic my limp and walk. I have limited range of motion in my leg. Sometimes I will see my reflection on a glass buildings of my walk, and it makes me feel a little sad. The truth 99% of the time, I am so thankful for my leg. I have become very quick and I have adapted well. I have always been a positive person, so I would try and apply that thought and I felt like I was in the ring of life, without any boxing gloves. I felt like I kept hitting the ground. In those situations, life becomes a filtering process and you are not the one who is in control of the filtering. The people who love you and are close to, move in closer. The ones you thought would be there and were not, move further away. I did not have the tools to deal with this at first but I eventually learned. There are many take a ways. I have learned from those days and still learning lessons today. We will talk about a degree from a university or college is important. I can tell you for sure the degree from University of Life is also important. I remember my first night going into the hospital to receive my first chemotherapy drug, I was petrified. On the drive, there I had a meltdown, "I am not going", I was crying and carrying on. When I got to the hospital, I remember basically signing my life away. Then I took off my clothes, my wedding ring and put on a hospital gown (someone like Ralph Loren needs to design a better version of those awful things). I felt like I was surrendering and giving myself over, losing control. I was put in a room with a man, who was truly suffering. The sounds, the smells of chemicals, and the moans, I will never forget. I was in despair that night. At about midnight, I got out of the bed, got my crutches. I hobbled down the cancer floor, while fluids dripped in my body to prepare me for the 4-hour drip of chemo in the morning. I looked out a window and saw how high up I was. I thought what if I just fell out the window, not jumped, but just fell. I really have not shared this before. I never had ever had that kind of despair before, I was scared, terrified and I felt so alone. I have never felt that way again. The lyrics of a song I wrote "Just Get Through The Night" came to mind "just get through the night, tomorrow with be alright". Always remind yourself there is always hope! Early the next morning a Doctor came into my room with several medical students. I was in bed and I heard the Doctor speak about my cancer and how bad my odds were. It was very matter of fact and I was treated like an experiment, a statistic. I did not say anything, but inside my thought was, not long ago I was just like you. The roller-coaster ride had just begun and the series of "shocks to the system" was just starting. Why do I mention all this? When I finished all my chemo treatments and all the physical therapy to learn to walk again, it was time to get a job that leads to a career!

    I am an overly optimistic and a positive person. I was excited to look at the next chapter of my life, when I finished all my treatments. I had this notion that someone would give me a chance with a job, just a chance. Then all I heard was the sound of crickets, silence. Remarks from Employers "What did you do the last two years...." "There looks like some large gaps in your resume". This was my journey on rebuilding the dream, finding hope again. It was very sterile, discouraging and a major let down. Words are ringing in my head, from what a co-worker said to me not to long ago, regarding getting a job. I had worked with him, in the IT space. I had recently been laid off after working for a company for many years. I moved from Florida to California to take a job with an IT company. The job was not a good career move and I was let go. This person had connections and good have helped me land a job. We were out to dinner and instead he had advice for me. He said the "world owes you nothing", this was in context to getting a job and life. He went on making his point I started to get teary, and we had to leave a restaurant. I do not cry easily, so you know this hit a nerve in me, many nerves. First, I disagree 100%. Sure no one owes anyone anything, but no one gets anywhere without help or being given a chance. Think about it, we first come into the world from the help of our mother. She carried us, nurtured us in the womb. Then our parents, clothed us, fed us, raised us. I don't necessarily disagree with his statement, but he left out the part, "the world owes you nothing, **BUT THANKFULLY SOME PEOPLE WANT TO HELP AND EXTEND YOU A GIFT, NOT DESERVED, A CHANCE**" and a dose of **GRACE**. That chance was given to me. Now flashback when finished all my treatments and no one was giving me the opportunity, I was in complete despair, very disappointed and very disillusioned, the world then felt heartless. Being on crutches, I was limited on what I could do. I wanted to contribute to taking care of my wife at the time and try rebuild a future together. With my now marriage always under pressure with a possible divorce, I did not know what to do. When I grew up and I still am, a huge fan of Donny Osmond, my brothers and I would perform his and other bands songs with family concerts. I wrote a letter to Donny, expressing how I was a fan and what I had gone through, I was not expecting a response.

With all my other attempts, there was no responses. He responded and offered me an internship/job and at that time he was in Southern California. I am so thankful to him and his manager Bill and Glen for giving me a chance. They sure did not need to and that time I felt like I had "Chemo Brain". People talk about this phenomenon when you finish chemo and it is so true. Now what was I saying, I just had a chemo brain relapse. It was an undeserved gift a chance offered. It gave me hope and inspiration. We partnered with an advertising company, where later I became Assistant to the President for this advertising agency in Newport Beach. We produced several national commercials during that time, and I was involved casting, location determination and production. Today Donny and Marie Osmond perform nightly in Las Vegas at the Flamingo. Think about it, even if you had the most stellar resume a company is still taking a chance on you and do not forget your taking a chance with them. We often forget, this is a two-way street, not a one-way street. This was confirmed when the concept of an "At Will" came to play. Basically, you can be let go or you can leave a company for any reason. The actual definition from the U.S Labor is "At-will" means an employee can be dismissed by an employer for any reason, without having to establish "just cause". Why did I include this, not to make a negative statement, but rather a positive one? Maybe it is just the way I think but, this brings freedom, from my perspective. Why? The way I look at a job or career, whether you work for a company or run your own, you still can view it the same way. Make your career decisions like you are the President or CEO. You might say, well that is not realistic, but it is. Your time is valuable commodity and you own that, not the company. This is not a selfish statement either. These are the rules of engagement, so we all work in those guidelines. I have seen many times; a person gets let go after working with a company for 25 years. This happens before it is retirement time also. A person I have high respect for, worked for a major IT manufacturer, she was a PBM (Product Business Manager), she actually took a chance on me and gave me my first IT job, representing hp as a Regional Sales Manager. I had never worked in this industry before. It was definitely taking a chance on me. She is amazing person at what she does and who she is and is well respected. All who knew her was shocked, how could this have happened. She could have been, knocked down and in despair, I am sure she was to some degree. Well she ended up with a competitor, in a higher position and she is Director of Distribution. The point is to know again the rules of engagement, work hard, be dedicated to the company, but also dedicated to yourself. When I went through my cancer experience, I learned life lessons, that are tattooed on me. I have well over 50 screws and metal in my leg, there is always a reminder, but also a reminder to be thankful every day. I now have a motto I live by **"every day is icing on the cake"**. Life is a gift. I want you all not to make my mistakes, believe me you will make your own. I thought I was going to have four kids, playing sell out concerts and traveling the world, a simple request (HAHAHA). I am divorced twice, my hair never grew back right after chemo, I have a limp, no children. What do I have, a smile on my face and the humble realization that people in this small world right now are going through so much more than me and time to get my eyes of me and never set the table for a pity party!I am an Uncle my brothers and families together are 12 nieces and nephews. Four are in college and soon to be entering the work force for careers. This is the same advice I would give my own kids; you know what still may not be too late for me. (This book is not intended to be filled with statistics, graphs or if you follow my plan in 3,000 days you will have your dream House, spouse and be completely fulfilled in your life guaranteed (please read the fine print for the disclaimer and it will be sped read at 90 miles an hour). I hope you see things through a hopeful lens and that you have fun in the process. This is a new concept for me, and it has been life changing. This desert oasis was created and is in constant development and improvement, the same way we should also be, always striving to be better and not just in monetary terms, but in life.

What I have learned, is to be open. In my early career, it was all about music. First as a performer, then in the music business and ironically, I end up in the IT industry. Which I have mentioned has been the best career decision so far. I don't look at life or a career as an all or nothing approach, to me it is about adapting and modifying, without compromising who you are. While I represented hp, I was a Product Specialist, Brand Evangelist (what a great title) and Regional Sales Manager, all wrapped in one. My territory was the western region from California, Seattle, Portland and every location a channel partner has a location. I worked with Major DRC Reseller and their Sales Representatives on selling my products for Hewlett Packard. My office was airports and airplanes. I had the opportunity to see almost the entire United States and Canada. I was always put up in the nicest hotels, like the Palmer House in Chicago and the W in Montreal. I would do sales training's for up to several hundred people at a time or smaller focus groups. I also created VIP events around music venues and featuring artists I had worked with in the past. I was not instructed to do these events, and these were not done on a whim. I was given a budget and I created the events ground up, like a Vegas production. I did not have larger budgets then co-workers for hp, so I had to be creative. One event I did was at a hotel called, The Hotel Valley Ho in Scottsdale, AZ. The event was a quarter event and the top sales reps, would earn a VIP night with them and a guest. It was an awesome night. I flew in a new known country/singer songwriter from Nashville, originally from Russia, she did an amazing job. Everyone received a signed CD(a cd is a silver disc that is interested into a player and music is produced- lol), catered dinner forms their chef on the top of the roof of the hotel with the views of Arizona mountains all around, on a warm summer night. It was an awesome night; it was done for a low budget with a very nice ROI (return on investment) for hp and the re-seller. The feedback was that it was one of the best events that this re-seller has seen. It was because of genuine passion I have for music and for people to succeed. I mention this because, sure I am working in IT, but I infused my love for music in the event. Find your passion, harness it, embrace it and incorporate it into what you do, this is your gift to the world. Other co-workers love sports, so that is there focus and they should also infuse their passion with , their occupation. I have been wanting you to get to know about me. We are in the chapters to follow, going to dive into the sparkling pools of Vegas. We are going to discover practical tips on getting a job and ultimately a career.

8

What Makes Vegas-Vegas: What Makes You-YOU!

"I've Gotta Be Me' This song was made famous by a great Vegas singer and dancer Sammy Davis Jr. He truly lived the lyrics. He overcame many obstacles; one was losing his left eye in a car accident. During his early career, there was also horrible racial prejudices, some performers would have quit and gave up, it never stopped him and his performing career just continued to excel. He became a member of the "Rat Pack" with Frank Sinatra, not a bad gig.. I've Gotta Be Me' is a phrase I wished I had asked myself. As I mentioned I was a different person going into the cancer experience and then the other side of it. One thing that stayed the same was I was always hopeful and that is who I was and that essence of me always remains. There were also changes that I had to learn to except. Recently a friend of mine was going through pictures of me in the past, he found in my storage unit. He got emotional and I admit it hurt. He was like "you were so much different". He was looking at all my concert photos, publicity pictures and my sports pictures. I am for sure a different person in many ways. I was very active, a swimmer, runner, skier and dreamer. I can still dream! The rest I am not able to do, as you know. I remember the first year after chemotherapy, my hair would fall out and then grow back again. Hands full of hair would be in my hands when I took a shower, in clumps. Soon it would grow back again. I had to have a second surgery on my leg because a plate broke, and it broke across the cadaver bone. As a result, I have limited range of motion in my leg. I have over 50 screws in my leg and metal plates, that go from my knee to my hip. How does all these changes make me feel, Thankful to God! It is not what I cannot do, it is about what I can do! Every day like I said before is "Icing on the cake" for me, really! Hopefully what we go through makes us better people, but that is always a choice. Las Vegas chooses to reinvent itself all the time and so did I. I will always have the scars and feel the screws in my leg to remind me of the painful chapters in my life. Las Vegas has old Vegas downtown, but it is in the rear-view mirror for both of us. One of my Phonoville songs is called **"Can't Rewind" "Stop. Pause Whats the cause of all our indecision Stop.Pause Whats the cause, what is left but division, cause you Can't rewind"**. Oh, I have tried, to recapture the past me, never to find that person. I have wanted a refund of time from a past relationship, but I cannot get that time back either. When I finished all my chemotherapy and I was learning to walk and using a walker and then crutches. I also lived many years with fear of the possible re-occurrence of the cancer. I have learned again by "Trial and Error" , to live one day at a time and there have been moments one second at a time.

    I think it is good to know your strengths and yes, your weaknesses. First question **"What Makes You-You"**? the good the bad and the ugly! Do a self-discovery evaluation. Find out your interests. What do you like to do? Get your list out again, what don't you like to do? Sounds basic, it is and it is just the beginning. Be observant with yourself and the people around you. **What do you have to offer, your gifts and talents?** When looking at Vegas, all types of jobs are available to you. Can you write, produce, can you promote, market, or sell? Can you create something, solve a solution to a problem? What is your personality type? Are you outgoing, quiet, energized when you're around people or are you more of an introvert and you recharge with alone time? There is the freeing with **"IT IS OKAY TO BE JUST WHO YOU ARE"** you are born unique, we just all need to be fined tuned. Think about any instrument, when not tuned it does not sound good, but everything you need to make a beautiful sound is there, just needs to be tuned up. This example to could be also made for a car, it needs to be maintained and tuned up regularly. Guess what it makes sense, all these things are made by people, why should we be any different. So many times, in my career pursuit, I tried to adapt and be whatever the available company position needed. The result would be getting fired or I would quit. The end result is loss of time and direction. We all grow and change, but I believe we are each a unique blueprint and who knows you best but you. Listen to yourself and be honest with your strengths and weaknesses. Learn from other people's mistakes and successes. Seek wisdom from others that have been there. Speak to retired people, that found their career path and their journey.

I have four other brothers and we are all wired differently. We each were born with a different personality trait and that applies also for twins. They say people can change, to a degree yes, but the core of who you are I don't think does. I am basically saying do not fight against it, embrace it. I am guilty of this and maybe you are also. I wish I were like that person or looked like that person or had a career like that person. What a waste of time, be you and you will find you!

If I were to ask you to create your own production for a Vegas show, **what would it look like?** (There is no wrong answer). Would you be the Talent, the featured Artist? Would you be the Promoter? Would you be a Creator? Would you be the Producer? What is the takeaway here, all these are operated by talented people in a variety of different roles and the combination of these talents are combined to make a successful production? Interesting and very cool! I will bet at the gambling tables of life, that one of these categories would be a perfect match for you. Think now about a Vegas production and all the roles involved and answer the question, who am I in this production, what is my contribution and my strengths. I think this simple task could be life changing. Think about "Love" the Beatles show in Vegas. First, I am a huge Beatles fan. As we mentioned all that needs to go into the show. Training the acrobats, being the acrobat/actor. The sound engineer, the advertiser, the promoter, the ticket agent, the managers, the booking agents, the creator of the concept/writer, set designer. Okay long winded yes, but so valuable to think this way. Then think about a corporate structure and process it the same way. Think about all the departments within the corporation. Research the company through online tools like Glassdoor and LinkedIn and Indeed. Send a resume and get that interview. One purpose for this book is to learn from my mistakes and to learn from my successes. One thought I always try to remember is I can always learn something new and be a better person for it. This is another theme to this book is always be in **"Learn Mode"**. My advice in take personality tests, take courses with the end goal purpose to define your fit in the workforce. Ask people what they think you are good at. It is helpful to get advice from people, but remember it is just an opinion, not a definition of who you are. Gather data, research career options, do internships, volunteer. A funny observation about volunteering or giving back. When we get our eyes off ourselves sometimes, that is when we can sometimes get true clarity about who we are and understand the world around us better. If you attend church, get involved, be on the worship team, be a greeter, help with the setup and tear-down. That applies with schools also. Seek out people you respect that are in businesses that you have an interest in. Interview them, ask about their journey. Get involved somewhere. It never hurts to ask, be curious and keep your eyes open wide. There are also so many great books available in being better at business. When an opportunity does come up, do the best you can, work hard at it. Some people think in an internship, I just need to do the basics because I am not getting paid for it, it is required for school. Work like you are being paid a great salary and it could turn into one. Everything you do whether it is positive or negative experience will follow you and ultimately affect your career choices and opportunities in the future. Be a bridge builder, do not sabotage or tear down it, especially while you are walking on it. Sometimes we get in our own way. I have gotten in my way many times.

Our society sometimes has the thought process of what's in it for me and there is a step missing and that is paying your dues. That may look different for everyone, but rarely do things just fall into place, there are steps and obstacles that come along the way. Sometimes doing a job, one realizes that it was not utilizing their strengths. Quick motto shows up a little early and leave a little bit late, if you do that you are already ahead of the curve.

I remember doing a series of interviews for a company based in San Diego. The recruiter told me that he has had several people show up twenty minutes late for the in-person interview and some were a no-show. The late interviewees even expected to still be interviewed, which they were not. One step that many forget is always send a thank you email after an interview. Do the extra things to standout. There is a mindset out there that a job is deserved not earned. I have always had to earn the work and that goes for colleagues I have worked with. The interview process can also be a marathon, not always a sprint.

The message here is BE YOU! at your best. Remember the two-way street. The company is interviewing you and in turn, you are interviewing them. Years ago, in an interview with a Southern California company. The VP of Sales gave a short introduction before the series of in person interviews that were to take place. In a very arrogant way, he said "I am the coach and you are the teammates". "All your prior sales experience stays outside these doors; I will train you my way or the highway". "With this job, I only hire Type A personalities". We were in a conference room of 15 people being interviewed. I spoke up after awhile and exhausted by his ranting and said, "I am not a type A personality, I am more of a B+ personality and I got up and walked out of the conference room interview". You have special talents; you may not always find the perfect job with all the right boxes checked but listen to your instincts and really assess yourself properly. Landing a bad fit job, just means you will be looking again in a short period of time for another job and a bad job choice, you leave, will follow you on your resume.

Everyone has challenges in life. Everyone travels a path and it leads in a certain direction. Many have clear direction on where it leads, however that route can be less common. The path on the Vegas strip, is filled with many options, distractions. Be alert and value your time, use it wisely. Then get ready for the lights, sounds and action of Vegas!

9

Vegas Is Selling-Everything Is Sales

I think this is a true statement. **"Vegas Is Selling, Everything Is Sales"**. First question why travel to Las Vegas? there are so many options out there. The other thought is Vegas is in the desert, not on a beach resort somewhere in the world. I guess that could be argued, since some of the resorts look like a beach setting-lol. Maybe soon they will import an ocean to this desert location. It is however the Oasis in the desert. It has grown and changed throughout the decades and has evolved into a one stop destination. One major aspect is sales. I would argue that Vegas is one of the best brands with their sales, it is the ultimate **"Sales Slot Machine"**, a jackpot win ! The Vegas 4-mile Strip can be overwhelming with the endless activity options and all are trying to get your attention through sales, promotions, and marketing. It is a long four miles as well. When I was dating my girlfriend from Colombia, she had never been to Vegas. I was on a business trip there. So what did we do. We got on Facetime and I walked most of the entire strip showing here the sights and sounds. It is a great memory for me. "Phono" was again being able to be a tour guide and I had a beautiful guest! Every year there are over 40 million visitors to this global destination. Why the appeal? I think there are many reasons. One is that Vegas has Universal appeal and is home of the **Las Vegas University of Selling!** (that part I made up)

The Sales are going on 24/7 and guess what, that is not always a negative thing. I would argue that we as culture adapt a sales concept to life and it is a worldwide appeal. The presidential debate I believe is also a form of sales. In the political arena the election of a President involves the parties selling their concepts and beliefs. The campaigns, the rallies throughout the United States is a form of sales. Even the television and radio spots for an upcoming election, are direct sales. Yes, the word "sales" has a taboo stigma, but the applications are ingrained in all of us. We may use different definitions, but the processes are the same and the results are accomplished, by sales.

Think for a moment about a definition of who Las Vegas is: Some attributes that comes to is, top notch entertainment in one place. Great food, the best resorts, one stop location the list goes on and on. Vegas is laser focused selling to the individual or group. Where will you eat, where will you stay, what will you do? Next, we all look at online reviews and people who give their opinions to either sell you on something or to sell you against, what could be a bad choice, in their opinion. It is amazing the power of influence of social media. Five-star reviews carry great merit, but a negative review does a lot of damage, to what is being reviewed. As the lights on the Vegas strip illuminate, you get all dressed up, put on the cologne, or perfume and get ready to hit the Vegas strip. You Definitely are selling you! Try and sell me, that you are not. Not buying it. LOL!

I learned for myself how to define what I like about sales and where is the best fit for me. My conclusion was I lean toward solution selling. I need to believe in what I am selling, whether it is a product or a service. I do not like the approach of selling something I do not find value in. Do not get hung up on the word, keep the approach natural and sell your personality. In the world people have been accustomed to saying an automatic "NO", regarding sales, many leave it at that point. Try and stick around and ask why? Many forget in the sales process; it is more important to listen than to speak. You want to understand what concerns, needs and what problems that can be solved. This is termed "Pain Points". Take it a step further, listen to yourself. Find out what are your pain points and what is holding you back from a career that will bring fulfillment to you.

The next question, what is **Your Definition**, who are you and what do you have to offer? Sales 101, before you can sell anything, you must know what you are selling. Then you must know the features and benefits of what you are selling. Then why is it better than the competition. Interesting how this applies to you, a job interview and to this place called Las Vegas.

What is your personality? Do you like to work with people or more at a task type role? Would you be a better manager of people or a manager of product? I am a people person; I rather be around people than alone. However, one career path I thought about being was a Psychologist. For years I thought this and took courses in that area. I am so happy I did not do this. I would have taken my work home and I would end up needing a Psychologist, to help me deal with being one. One job that does not appeal to me now is to be a Manager of People, a manager of product yes, not people. Again I like to be around people, and I am a people person but just not in a management role, which involves things like HR issues.

These concepts are also supported with Vegas. Each hotel/resort has a theme and a customer profile. Some are geared toward families, others toward couples or singles. When we choose the hotel, food, and entertainment we run it though our **"Likes Filter"**. As you can see, we are all accustomed to doing this kind of evaluation or series of processing all the time. Sometimes we forget to take the time to step back and acknowledge why we make those kind decision or choices. My suggestions when looking for a career, let it stream naturally like you would choosing a song you want to hear or band you want to see live. Try and be honest and natural. I would focus more on the "not a good fit" and leave room open for the possible "good fit". What I have learned, is to be open. In my early career, it was all about music. First as a performer, then in the music business and ironically, I end up in the IT industry. Which I have mentioned has been the best career decision so far. I don't look at life or a career as an all or nothing approach, to me it is about adapting and modifying, without compromising who you are. While I represented hp, I was a Product Specialist, Brand Evangelist (what a great title) and Regional Sales Manager, all wrapped in one. My territory was the western region from California, Seattle, Portland and every location a channel partner has a location. I worked with Major Reseller's and their Sales Representatives on selling my products for Hewlett Packard. My office was airports and airplanes. I had the opportunity to see almost the entire United States and Canada. I was always put up in the nicest hotels, like the Palmer House in Chicago and the W in Montreal. I would do sales training's for several hundred people at a time or smaller focus groups. I also created VIP events around music venues and featuring artists I had worked with in the past. I was not instructed to do these events, and these were not done on a whim. I was given a budget and I created the events ground up, like a Vegas production. I did not have larger budgets then co-workers for hp, so I had to be creative. One event I did was at a hotel called, The Hotel Valley Ho in Scottsdale, AZ. The event was a quarter event and the top sales reps, would earn a VIP night with them and a guest. It was an awesome night. I flew in a new known country/singer songwriter from Nashville, originally from Russia, she did an amazing job. Everyone received a signed CD(a cd is a silver disc that is interested into a player and music is produced- lol), catered dinner forms their chef on the top of the roof of the hotel with the views of Arizona mountains all around, on a warm summer night. It was an awesome night; it was done for a low budget with a very nice ROI (return on investment) for hp and the reseller. The feedback was that it was one of the best events that this reseller has seen. It was because of genuine passion I have for music and for people to succeed. I mention this because, sure I am working in IT, but I infused my love for music in the event. Find your passion, harness it, embrace it and

HOW TO GET A JOB VEGAS STYLE

incorporate it into what you do, this is your gift to the world. Other co-workers love sports, so that is there focus. Try not to cut corners. I have a few times booked a hotel in Vegas because it was cheap. It was a compromise and I ended up paying more, to compensate for the mistake. I think with the initial filter, you will know, what is not a good fit regarding a job or career. It is like seeing a show in Vegas because everyone around is writing great reviews. You think nothing about "does this has an appeal to me". But Hey! if everyone around recommends it, it must be good. You go and the night is a course in endurance. This action item calls for being honest with yourself and being realistic. It could be compared to auditioning for a musical in Vegas, but you can't sing or dance. You are waiting in line and your next to go for your try out and all you can think is "why am I here".

Everything is also geared toward getting the best deal or best value. We as a consumer are very savvy at this, with concepts like "President Day" Sales and the list goes on. Let us do a quick illustration. You are planning a relaxing trip to there. Well just the planning of the event, you will need a vacation from that experience. Everyone involved in the process is selling you on what airline, hotel, food, and entertainment to indulge your senses. If you think about sales , it can be an exhausting process, or it can be very natural. The reality this is our world. I went a Jr, College before I attended UCLA. My focus was Marketing and Music, the M&M degree (BTW, there is a great M & M store on the Vegas Strip. I like the M & M's with nuts, how about you?). What I learned early on and throughout my career, is marketing, products, inventions, concepts and the first important is yourself, it all requires SALES.

Just like before you plan a trip to Vegas, you must decide on Vegas first, then all else follows suit.

I learned in Marketing courses, I could spend a lot of time creating a great marketing concept, but without the vehicle of sales, it goes nowhere.

Sell yourself first. To sell anything, you must know what and how to sell the product YOU!. Everything is defined by sales, if you are providing a product, service, or solution, this involves selling. The shows in Vegas are created, crafted and designed for mass audiences. The shows are also cutting edge, with state-of-the-art technology, which involves lights and sound. They also have top notch talent and not just the performers, but all aspects of production. We can learn by just observation that it is an effective proven method for Las Vegas shows, this can also be directly applied to you. First know who you are and who you are not. This process of defining yourself will save you a lot of frustration. Remember there are lots of different productions in Vegas as we have spoken before in previous chapters, you just need to find your perfect show. I mentioned before, I really believe that everyone has some talents and gifts. The challenge is that many follow after other people's talents and gifts and ignore what they have within themselves, which is the perfect fit. Look at it this way. You are at the Hard Rock Hotel and your favorite band is about to perform, their guitar player is a no show. They ask you if you would fill in on guitar and you agree. Your thought is I have seen some YouTube videos for guitar, how hard can it be. As you approach the stage, you realize "wait I do not play at all" as you walk on stage before the crowd...... then you wake up is a sweat! My point is there is many aspects that makes a person who they are. When you are selling, promoting, and marketing yourself, make sure you know that the product you are selling and again it is You. Take the time to self-reflect and define yourself. First be honest and ask friends and family who you trust, what they think. Then process the information, use a filtration approach, because it is your life ultimately, it is not recommended to live in the shadow of someone else. I have made the mistake of trying to force something to work and it was clearly a bad fit. Las Vegas A job is a performance and each quarter you will be judged on performance, by the company.

    I remember working for a major national retail vitamin company. I would be the only manager at night, it was one of my first experiences in sales. I would educate and sell supplements and vitamins to our Newport Beach customers. One night I took out food from the health-conscious restaurant chain called McDonald's. I was preparing for a night of food coma. I ordered A burger, six piece of chicken Mc Nuggets, large fry, and a coke to wash it down. I brought the food into the back office. In between selling health products, I would indulge in my dinner. So halfway into my meal, while my eyes were starting to close, the district manager showed unannounced and walked into the back office, while I was in the middle of processing a series of fries and a Mc Nugget at the same time. She was in shock and I was bright red embarrassed. She was the picture of heath, a vegetarian, she lived the healthy lifestyle completely. My philosophy that night was fill the food void. This was the moment that defined my future jobs and they would be in sales. I said without missing a beat, "I am doing a test to see how fast food affects work productivity" No she did not believe it and I thought was that the best response I could come up with. So, my future would have to be a salesman, like pay it forward, no more like payback. My point is believing in what product or concept you are selling. Then ,Why should someone hire you? What do you have to offer? Please do not say personality, that job aspect is not paying well these days. As we have discussed the term sales has such bad connotations; however, everything requires it. The most incredible marketing plan needs sales to implement the program effectively. I have heard all the negative sales terms "Turn and Burn", "Smile and Dial" and the list goes on. There is a term I do like is Solution Selling, this is identifying and providing a solution that would benefit the customer. There is nothing wrong with uncovering a potential customer's pain point. Look at yourself and come up with positive statements. Choose words like dedicated, hardworking, creative, caring, positive, words that can pertain to you. Everyone has something positive, search for them and be honest. Now all of these are desirable attributes that a company would look for. My job path has been very reactive in the past, notice I term it as a "job" and not saying career. Choose a career direction and don't be in auto pilot mode, know when to stay in a job and when to leave. Always try and leave on a good note. Your resume is the pathway to where you will settle ultimately in a career. It is the road map to where you have been and going in your career direction. A lot of my resume roads have been under-construction and there were many detours.

Stereotypes from the past of the used car salesperson, telemarketers, door to door sales and the list goes on. Corporations have incorporated new positions to change the sales negativity's. New positions like "Customer Success Specialists" and one of my positions when I represented hp was "Brand Evangelist", "Product Specialist" and a more common term "Regional Sales Manager". Do not let the titles fool you, every "quarterly review" we had to exceed our quarter quota, which again translates to net new sales. I had a telemarketing job in San Diego years ago. I started at 6 am and end at 3:30 pm. We would put on our headsets and the system would automatically call the person at their home. There was never a ringing period between calls. After Hanging up with a call automatically the next person would be on the call. It was beyond awful. Not only was it not a welcomed call but I was selling "When animals attack" videos and other similar themes and no I am not kidding. It became "When Telemarketers are attacked by uninterested People". That might sell, note to self. The other terrible part, all the calls were recorded, you and your manager would review them at the end of the day. Not only did you get verbally assaulted on the phone, your manager was able to add to the already lovely day. If your career does not directly deal with sales, you will be working in some way with sales within an organization. To understand sales is at least an important thought. You are the product and your product is something you live with all the time. Own your uniqueness, there is a fit somewhere for you, so try not and get discouraged. Selling can be fun. Think about the advertisements for a new movie coming out or the lighted billboards on the Vegas strip. The producers are trying to sell you to see the film and it is presented in a captivating way. Selling also requires skill and tools and both are ongoing and never perfected. Find a job or career that is a good match for you. Then sell your skills and experiences. If you act, take more acting classes, learn the craft by reading up on those actors you admire. Learn from others and be the best salesperson you can for yourself. You can avoid and try and go only with natural talent, but that will only get you so far. Even as a musician, you may be the best at what you do, it still helps to understand the music business and how to present and sell your music. I have heard the phrase, "It will sell itself", yeah right! That advise will not get you far and it will be reflected in your bank deposits, from that kind of advice. Sales knowledge can't hurt but can really help. Remember someone bought desert land in the middle of nowhere and it has been making a profit in record sales ever since. It is now a destination on prime property. **"You Are Prime Property, Time To Sell You"**!

10

A Job Is A Performance

A job is a Performance and each quarter or whatever metric your company uses, you will be judged on performance, by the corporate. Just like in school a progress report. I have made this mistake before. I was hired by a well know IT product manufacturer. The Director of Distribution got me hired in a role, that was all numbers and spreadsheets. The idea was getting me in the door and when a sales role opens, then transfer to that position. I did not realize it was a revolving door. I was out of my element and we mutually agreed the job was not a fit. It was a time of great stress. I grew up with a learning disability called dyslexia. I was so over my head and the stress were off the rector scale. My job there was all stats and math. Some would love this, like my older brother. I was in the right company, but the wrong place. Remember they only know what you tell them. There are times when you may apply for a job, but the HR team thinks you're a better fit in another department. Communication is key. I used to be a skeptic on taking personality tests and that they were limiting. Now I believe they are an effective tool, not a definition of who you are but a broad idea. Myers Briggs is a good test. I am a ENFP (Extrovert, Intuitive, Feeling and Perception). One of my brothers is CEO of a company in this space, he works with PI "Predictive Index". They offer a great tool for companies and their employees. This kind of knowledge really has been helpful to know, how to work within the framework of your personality. What is interesting, I think we are born with these traits to some degree. If you have brothers and sisters, you can see this in real time. I have four brothers and we are all different, yet we all grew up in the same home, with the same parents. My point is trying to embrace who you are, work with your gifts, not against them. We all have strengths and weaknesses. The more you know YOU the better you will be in a work environment. Remember even that can be taken to extreme, it is about balance. I believe the core of who you are is basically in your DNA, I would say **God Given**. Sure, life changing circumstances can alter that, but the essence of who you are is there. I have done many jobs that were definitely not a right fit for me, and I did it anyway. Also, you know yourself better than anyone else does. What someone says it is the right job for you, it really may not be. If it is, you will know. I find it real funny during the "corporate dating period" the lets get to know you period. The interviewer first approach, is what a great fit you would be. Every time I would fall for, "they really like me' syndrome. Wow I can do no wrong. Then after the process, an email arrives. "We have moved onto a candidate with more of the qualities we were looking for" . Then my thoughts would be , "they did not like me", "we only had two corporate interview Dates". I wrote a song called **"Its Over"** , **"Its over before its begun, its over like the setting sun"**. Like I said its corporate "speed dating". Try the old school approach make a list of pros and cons. Find your interests and identify them. Determine is this a job that requires a degree or not. (later will be a chapter called (**To Degree or Not Degree, That Is the Question**). Map out your career. Like we discussed earlier, it takes many people to put on a production in Las Vegas. It requires talent in all departments, where do you fit. Now no career or job is perfect, but if you find your place in a company, at least in the right area, you can find your way. I know of a large company, when you are employed by them, it is important, you get a role within an area of interest. The next step is to make sure the manager, will promote. In this case they have control of you moving up in the organization, they also control if you want to move to another division. The thought again is to understand how to position yourself and how to present yourself. Both terms are used when selling something. You are the product and your product are something you live with. Own your uniqueness, there is a fit somewhere for you, so don't get discouraged. Selling can be fun. Think about the adverts for a new movie coming out. The producers are trying to sell you to see the film and it is presented in a captivating way. Selling also requires skill and tools and both are ongoing and never perfected. Find your uniqueness and then match it with skills needed. If you act, take more acting classes, learn the craft by reading up on those actors you admire. Learn from others and be the best salesperson you can. You can avoid and try and go with natural talent, but that will only get you so far. Even as a musician, you may be the best at what you do, it still helps to understand the music business and how to present (sell) your music. I have heard the phrase, "It will sell itself", yeah right. That advise won't get you far nor will the bank deposits you will get from that kind of advice. The **Guitar Fairy** will fly with its guitar and drop money from the sky into the back of musicians amps. Yes, I know that has happened before, but the **Guitar Fairy**, seems to be on tour all time these days. Also the **Tooth Fairy** seems to get all the PR attention. Sales knowledge can't hurt but can really help. Remember someone bought desert land in the middle of nowhere and it has been making a profit in sales ever since.

11

Vegas Is A Brand: Brand=You

Our society globally is brand driven, from what you wear, what you listen to your music on, where you go, what you see, where to stay. Brand, Brand and (Boy Bands) wait no Brand lol. Naturally if everything around revolves around brand then also applies to you. My ex-wife is in the apparel industry. She worked for the top brands globally, which included Director of product for Nike, product manager for Reebok, Vans, North Face, and the list goes on. She ended up as a VP for a large urban brand of apparel. Now I would say these were dream jobs and I lived vicarious through her and I did. We had amazing discussions on brand direction, selling the brand, merchandising, and developing innovations. During our marriage I worked with all the major and independent record labels in Los Angeles and a few based in Nashville. The labels were Warner Brothers, Maverick, Universal Music Group and their labels like Geffen, A & M, Universal South Island etc. My job was a combination of Promotions, Sales and Branding. I would compile compilations with a variety of Artists. We would combine and produce CD's that would go to independent stores and college campuses. Locations like restaurants tattoo parlors, coffee shops etc., They would play the music in rotation throughout the day, we also included a magazine, that featured the artists on the compilations. I now have very nice collection of eclectic cd's. The record labels found tremendous value in this business model, so I would have an open door with marketing and A & R staff. This is a form of branding/marketing called "Guerrilla Marketing" and I love it because I believe it produces results. This form of branding gets to the consumer directly, you receive the pulse and gut reaction with your fan right away. The complication we created would feature new artists teamed up with current artists. I promoted new bands on the same CD from Paul McCartney to Radiohead. How does this relate. You are the artist and you need to be on the CD ok Mp3 alright Spotify. Seriously as I state with my company "audiolution" tm **"You Have A Voice, Use It"**. Dream big and see where it takes you. Surround yourself around the industries and people you respect. Always be a student of your craft, this will define you as the Brand. Brand is a concept and lifestyle and it is genuine. I do not believe Brands survive unless they are true representations. Surfers like "Quiksilver" runners etc. like "Adidas". Be an authentic brand, be yourself, the best version of YOU! I worked for a successful pet products company as a Western Regional Manager. I worked the CEO of the company directly. We would fly across my region and meet our accounts; he was also the pilot and a crazy one at that. On one of many trips he told me a story. He said he did a sales contest with our distributor sales representatives. It was a big production and it lasted for a quarter period. After the contest ended, there was an award ceremony. The winners were called up to the podium and were presented a Rolex watch. I heard it was an emotional event, some of the winners had tears from the emotional event. About a month later, one of the sales reps brought the Rolex watch to an authorized Rolex dealer for repair, he was told it was a fake. The CEO became then silent and so did I. How horrible all around I thought and then the CEO started laughing, he knew they were fake the whole time." **Be An Authentic Brand!!** " On a positive note, we were early on helping veterinary clinics and hospitals establish retail centers in their facilities. This was a new concept for Veterinaries at the time. We stated, you have the trust of your customer, why not sell them their veterinary services, pet food and accessories as well, instead of them getting it all from a large pet store chain. It was an incredible solution and yet many did not get it or see the value. Soon after being educated they got the concept. You see in every industry, sales is important but also brand is key as well! We all have many parts to our body and all the parts have a role and a function. The same applies to You as a Brand. Be early adapters, like mentioned in this book find your place in this production of life. Las Vegas has established themselves, but are constantly refining and perfecting their Brand. We all have talents and gifts, find yours. Dream big, but also be a little realistic, but keep it balanced. Always be open and step up to the plate. When you sit down at the blackjack table, there is elements of risk. Sometimes it is an important move to make a change and show the cards you have been dealt. I have learned this firsthand. I stayed with an IT company, because I liked my position, while colleges around me were making job changes and expanding their careers with new opportunities. I ultimately got laid off after seven years. Inside I was thinking how loyal I was to this company. There were thousands laid off nationwide, so it was not personal. What I learned, when you sign the documents of employment there usually is the term "at will", which states, the company can let you go at any time. It also means that you can advance or change your career when it is best for you and or your family. There is a term called "Independent Contractor" or "Self Employed". I believe we should think this way, you are your own brand or corporation. Companies today for the most part are looking out for their best interests and so should you. Great work ethic never changes however, just your perspective. When you are at a gambling table in Vegas, you usually don't put all your chips down on your first round of Blackjack. On this subject also be careful when signing a non-compete clause and the length of time of the contact, that you cannot work for a competitor, they are a binding agreement and some companies with enforce it. Remember **"Risk equals Benefit"**. This is a running theme of mine and quote I have used throughout my life and this book. I will go a little deeper, believe in yourself, step out and be vulnerable, yes that is a risk also but, it could have life changing results. The point is branding is important and so are you. With all the companies I mention in this chapter, we can say, they have brand awareness and you know what they represent and who there are and their target markets. Would you say "I could have had a Nike; don't they make a diet cola version also". Isn't their slogan "Just Drink It". You know if they did develop a drink, I am sure it would do well, because of their history of brand awareness and brand development. That is branding, name recognition and brand identification. Now in terms of Las Vegas, they are genius at it!

Let us build on that thought, you are planning a trip to Vegas. Everything comes to mind, some conscious and some sub-conscious. What are you going to pack, what brands of clothes do you like, sunglasses to wear, toothpaste type, suntan lotion and the list goes on? Then what airline to get there with and what is that brand of that American Airlines, Delta, Southwest etc., the brand for the rental car, the hotel you will be staying at, the entertainment you will see. There is a point to all this listed. We have been condition to think this way naturally, right. When you list it out, it is exhausting, but this is all done without much thought, almost naturally. When you see Cirque du Soleil or Beatles LOVE, it is a brand of entertainment. When thinking of branding who are you? I would not recommend in the corporate world to be a symbol, like Prince did, now its certain fields, why not! I look at this exercise in a way of getting what is inside you and getting it out to your forefront. What are your passions, interests, hopes, and dreams? Do this and paint with big brush strokes. Editing if needed will come later. For me, I tend to be my worst critic. Can you imagine Elton John saying before his Red Piano show in Vegas, well this is going to suck! I know he is excited and thrilled every night. I am a huge fan of his catalog of music. He and Bernie Taupin did write "Rocket Man" and "Someone Save My Life Tonight" true classics! It is okay to believe in yourself and don't get in your own way. When I represented Hewlett Packard(hp) for over seven years. I was first responsible for the Western Region and the South East region. I was a product specialist but I also a "Brand Evangelist". I had never heard that term before. What I did was represented first hp, then my product lines. The role included managing trade show booths.

Product sales training's for large sales groups of a hundred or more, to smaller sales focused groups, both for end-user customers and reseller representatives. I was measured by sales growth. Without going too far off track, I look back and think how I went from the music industry to the IT industry. Now I should answer my question. The music industry has changed quite a bit, and everybody knows this fact, we have gone from 8 tracks, reel to reel, Cassettes, Vinyl, CDs to mp3, mp4, to cloud and streaming technologies. If you think about it, it all has happened in a relatively short period of time. In the 80's there was still vinyl records then progressed to cd's. The music industry has always been known for being extremely competitive and being in control of the music industry, it was like the "Hollywood Castles" in the Kingdoms of Los Angeles Hills. There is so many college students that get internships and work for no or minimal pay. I felt like a ping pong game, I was bounced in and bounced out of this industry. I always dreamed of being in the music business, first as an artist, then second in promotions or marketing or A & R. As mentioned before, I was in the process of landing a record deal, when I was diagnosed with Osteosarcoma (bone cancer). I guess you could say, I was at the craps table in Vegas and I put all my chips on music and lost the gamble at the time. That is how I felt then and honestly sometimes still do. That was my Plan A, I had no other options. I was newly married and facing bad odds and possible death, divorce, financial issues, relocation. As I mentioned and in my 20's. My goal during my treatments was to sing and write music. It was not a reality because I was extremely sick from the chemo. I was classified as disable, the irony was not because I was on crutches with my leg and being in traction, but because of the severity of the chemotherapy. During this process of cancer treatments and spending most of my days in hospitals and clinics. I lost who I was, my brand identity was completely gone. I was still being branded, but not by me. What was my brand a "Victim", "Helpless"not only by words but also by definition, but I felt it to my core, like permanent like a tattoo. This was negative branding. Having hope is important, **"Hope is the Gas that gets you to your** Dreams".

As I mentioned previously, it took a long time to regain my voice. For years it would just cut off randomly while speaking. It also took years, to learn to walk without a cane. My dreams were crushed, my momentum was over. Other differences were my goals also changed. A music career was no longer the most important prospect, it was simple prayer -to live. Many of you can relate, when your health goes, first thing is first getting well! The small victories are now big victories then. I also learned about human nature. When I was in a band for years in the past, starting in high school. We played large events and had fans. I really enjoyed it. We were in a popular Christian band at the time and it was a blessing to sing about God and to play music. I tried to practice what I sang about. I had never experienced health problems then, life was great. The point is, when I was going through chemo, I lost all my hair everywhere and I mean everywhere including my eyelashes. I became skin and bone. I remember my mom driving me home from a chemo treatment, my mom is awesome, she has always been very supportive. I was sitting in the passenger seat, and I was vomiting nonstop in a basin, as we were driving home. A car with four guys in it, kept speeding up to laugh and make fun of me. I was made fun of many and was told I looked like a plucked chicken or a "friendly alien". Flashback we used to play for thousands of people and after the show, some would even want my autograph. That person is gone and has never returned since. I am forever a different a person. I lost friendships during this time; lifelong career dreams gone. Music successes now looked a lot different to me, whether I liked it or not. I was growing up and learning tough and valuable lessons. Back to you as a brand. You see it not all about monetary benefits, all though that helps. It is about what excites you when you get up in the morning. Most of your life is a job or hopefully a career. Next important aspect is what is your mission statement pertaining to you, the **YOU Corporation**. Take a moment, you are going to be featured across from the Mirage on a large billboard. What are you going state about yourself? Who are you? What are gifts and talents you want (we all have something) to showcase? What makes you stand out? What are your passions? Be-

HOW TO GET A JOB VEGAS STYLE

come secure in yourself not in what you do or where you work. It used to be there was job security with the ability to climb the corporate ladder. Today it is more like the corporate elevator and there are blocked floors and sometimes the ride gets you to the basement where the exit is. In this environment be a team player, hard worker, but also be independent, self-reliant and resilient also. These rules of engagement are mandated from the company, but to also work smart and not to be naive is good business. I was laid off from a job from a person that was mentoring me, first I had to train for months my replacement, it was a major let down. Our whole team was eventually laid off, including the Director who managed me. Think about a Vegas show, all the costumes, lights and presentation are key. Dress for success, but I would take it a step further, incorporate you in it. It sounds silly, but I have done this. I have worn suits and shirts that were not me and I was uncomfortable. No performer in Vegas would get on stage and look like they just rolled out of bed. Now there have been times in when I have been in Vegas and I felt like I just rolled out of bed, for the entire day, but I did not show it. Vegas work events tend to have interesting effects the next day. One reason "open bars". I know it all sounds basic, but it is important to check off the list, when comes to self-branding. Preparation is another key to branding. Can you imagine a guitar player or vocalist doing a show in Vegas and saying I am going to wing it, I don't need to practice or know the chord structure or lyrics or melody, I got this. Talk about, never forgetting that show and it's called "One Night Only"! To prepare, includes your resume and the content and structure of it. At least three questions to ask the interviewer and to prepare on the questions you may be asked. Like with a Vegas show there are try outs and competition, how will you stand out in your audition. If you do these basic brand concepts we have discussed, you already are ahead of the game. you know it is kind of like a game. The interviewer really does not know if you will be a good fit or not, it's a gut reaction and really a gamble. You are also taking a gamble, because your time committing, is valuable, especially if right around the corner is a better fit career opportunity. We all only have so much time. Most of what we have discussed is backstage, it is the anticipation, preparation, and the rehearsal for the upcoming performance, called the interview. Now the adventure or maybe the sitcom or drama then begins, with this stage show call work!

12

Prepare For The Vegas Performance

I think about all the time and the effort people put into before a performance. When I was in elementary school, Jr. High, and High School, I was in various musicals, band concerts and choir performances. All of them and the teachers understood, it takes practice. There is a percentage of gifted talent, but there is always room for improvement. I would propose that life is a process of striving to improve and grow as a person, at least we strive for that. Think about the shows you were in while at school or even right now. It was never here is your script, songs to sing or sheet music, or you have 10 minutes, learn it because the show starts in 20 minutes. It is a process of rehearsal, preparation to get ready for your debut. I find it interesting that so many almost wing it for a job interview, I have seen people all the time, they show up any without preparation. When I see a show in Vegas, like recently Lionel Richie, it was top notch great show. All details were covered, the musicians were awesome, the song choices were great, and the show was effortless. Effortless how can that be, simple Preparation. The more you prepare, the less you have to worry about. I think sometimes one can confuses preparation as not being natural or not spontaneous. I may have been guilty of this early on, what is the balance between natural and over produced. The conclusion I have found is the more prepared you are, the more natural you become. It is like the foundation is laid, so you can build you, your own

Vegas hotel or show. Now preparation does not mean conform to what everyone else doing, adapting to the recent trends, you never want to lose yourself. In a musical or play. Each actor reads from the same script and if you see the same show a different night, the interpretation from another actor is different. Yes, the same songs, same words but different delivery. Preparing is just the foundations to build and create your unique performance. Have you ever seen or known somebody that tries to be too much like another musician or actor, it is an impossible task, I think? I was a lead singer for many years and as mentioned before we played some large gigs, but I was terrified of Karaoke. The only time I have ever done it is at a bar, is with a few drinks in my system. I don't enjoy it usually. People that know me, cannot understand this, it does not make sense to them, because I love to sing. I just don't think I can do justice like the original artist. I have however seen some amazing interpretations by other singers. I have also heard drunk people making fun of the person who is singing karaoke. They are the same people, who would never try, the unpaid critics. Do not waste your time with critics or opinions. This is a lesson that took me years to learn. Be your unique self-first, grow as a person and try to be a better you. Working in the music business, I have seen a lot of personalities and egos. An observation I found, I am not saying that it is always a fact, so take it any way you want. I found a lot of the newer bands had more attitude or egos than some of the classic well-known artists. I would see these new bands and it would be there first or second record and they thought they "were all that". Then I would see an artist/musician who has proven themselves for years that really "were all that"! Many are humble, thankful and they had grown as a person. I was truly fortunate to have spent a day with Johnny Cash in Southern California, work with John Waite on promotion of his more recent records and hung out with him at the Fillmore in Los Angeles. I have spent time with Paul Rodgers, I was promoting an opening band for him in San Diego and in San Francisco. I have promoted records for Dolly Parton, Paul McCartney (Lifelong Fan since a kid) Roland Orzabal from Tears for Fears and Joe Strummer, to name only a few. All are legends in the music industry. These were great experiences and memories and they happened after my cancer experience. It took many years of persistence and never giving up on my passion and goals. I have seen newer bands self-destruct, giving into the pressures of the lifestyle, and indulging into drugs, egos and the list goes on and end up with only one or two records. These bands had the best labels, best producers and they were talented. They always say a band is like a marriage, so true. What I have learned in a marriage, you must be careful not to lose yourself. It is two individuals becoming one, but you need to always be the you that you are! I find it tragic in a marriage or a dating relationship when one tries to change the other person. Sometime the transformation is successful. Then the one that wanted the change, no longer respects that person. I have seen this happen often. There is nothing wrong with preparation in all you do for a career of interest. This sets the stage to allow for freedom to follow, it is the platform for you to really shine on who you are. Let's imagine you are in Los Angeles, you and your friends think, let's drive to Las Vegas and you get in the car to drive. How do we get there? The response we will just drive, it will happen. You need to know where you are going, at least some direction. There is nothing wrong with also being realistic, but not to realistic. It is all about balance. Look at all the amazing shows like "O" at the Bellagio, what talent to pull off all those feats. I think the first hurdle to get through, is getting over the fear of heights. I would never be able to do any of that, one is I had major surgery on my leg, so it is impossible, however I would love to promote the show, create the promo material, to get people to see this amazing production. In this case you do need many cooks in the kitchen, and everyone should be working off the same cookbook or lifebook! Although creating a Sushi/Pizza hybrid restaurant could be an intriguing concept. Remember preparation can be a solo concept, but ultimately it needs to be grafted into working with others, in a stage show or the stage of the corporation. Think about the corporation as a show. If that is the case, I have seen some interesting shows, comedies, dramas, and many sitcoms. Some are still having running seasons today and there are lot have reruns, that had their season and the company is gone. Have you ever noticed or worked in company and asked yourself, how do they stay in business? It seems like what they are doing is counterproductive. I have also been around and have worked for the top corporations that have a global presence, that are doing a lot of right practices. I have been under training and leadership from PepsiCo Corporation, Hewlett Packard, PacBell, Dell, iHeart Radio, Universal Music Group and the list goes on. I have the privilege to be in training from the leadership of several of these impressive companies. It is a comforting take away that no company or person is perfect, so we and them are all in the same boat. We strive for perfection and we all fall short. In the process it is mind, body and spirit . Now breath, be calm, as I begin to panic more, while I try to stop worrying or worrying about trying to calm down. Seriously being healthy in all aspects makes for a better you. The goal is a **Better You**, to be a **Better Team Member**, not just to be self -reliant, although that has its place. Filtering is something I am learning and processing all the time. Who are you surrounding yourself around? Who are your peers and friends, do they build you up or tear you down? Are they a good influence or a bad influence? I have seen all at work events in Las Vegas this in action. Even at these work environment events, peer pressure to drink more or to participate in destructive behavior, can lead to damaging not only yourself but your career. I have heard of tragic things happening at these types of events. One was an event at a happy hour, a manufacturer representative was drinking with co-workers, most were staying at the hotel, where the event was taking place. Large amounts of alcohol were consumed. This co-worker was later left alone, and he went to drive home on his motorcycle. He never made it and as he was passing away, he was speaking to his girlfriend on his cell phone, the sirens were on their way, to late, what a tragedy! No peer pressure does not go away even after college and one bad decision can ruin your life or someone around you, or someone you love. Prepare for this and surround yourself with people that love and care for your best interest. Also be the person that loves and cares

HOW TO GET A JOB VEGAS STYLE

for their best interest. It is a two-way street always. I have learned many valuable lessons, some I wished were not true, but you cannot live in a false shelter. A little more detail when I joined the fraternity at UCLA, I decided to live in the house. My justification was it is a large school and I need to get plugged in. I came to UCLA after being in A Christian band. I had a crash course in the other side of the spectrum. Everything I stood for was challenged, it was a very tough time. I never really drank before and then I was drinking to avoid peer pressure, to the point of alcohol poisoning and academic probation my first quarter and the nickname "Gumby". These people were called your brothers, friends "Fraternal". Fast forward to my chemotherapy days, that was only a year and a half after UCLA. How many of my bros from the fraternity called me to see how I was? How many asked how I was doing? How many sent a card. The answer Zero! I remember one day my ex-wife at the time was down in La Jolla one day to take a break, it was always a production with the crutches and the large leg brace. I was of course underweight, no hair and wearing a cap. As we walked down by the water, three of my fraternity brothers were walking on the street toward us. It was so out of context because this was San Diego. I had known them from Los Angeles it was uncomfortable and awkward completely, without a doubt. It was two different worlds and now we would collide. They were partying having a great time, they had not changed, and I had changed profoundly, even if I had not opted to, this was my new reality. There was no real conversation because they were uncomfortable, by my appearance. I felt like the character Beast, from Beauty and the Beast. I felt ugly! It was a short exchange, as they walked by I began to sing one of the songs from that musical. No, I did not do that. Don't you know me by now? Well, with me that could be a possibility. No numbers were exchanged and I never heard or have seen from them again. I had another friend at the time, that kept asking how I got it, he was so worried that cancer was contagious. I did not see him until long after my treatments were finished, our friendship did not last. There was no resentment, but he missed a large part of my life and whether I liked it or not I was different and really, he had not changed. The truth is that the people that remained in my life were my core family and close friends that were with me all along. There is no Gage in a friendship or about how that should look. Simple gestures go a long way. Again, this is not intended to be critical of these people, they are in different places and no one is required to be there for me, it is a choice, not a requirement. I find preparation being close to identification. Who you surround yourself is important? Having the same goals, morals and ethics is all important. This means the company you work for you needs to find value in similar things. Picture yourself working for a cause you completely disagree with and say hey it is for a paycheck. I do not think many would do this or at least without having some detrimental outcome. Listen to wisdom, learn from others, find a mentor. People for the most part want to help, surround yourself around them. Find friends that truly support you and again then returning support to them is mutual, otherwise that's not a true friendship. Guard your heart. I used to not like the term, "boundaries" but it is important to apply these principles to distance yourself from toxic people, unless there is a true cry for help. Human nature is interesting, and history does repeat. How many times do people make the same mistakes and not learn from them? How many times have people been given chance after chance and they reject it? A person on the outside thinks if I had that opportunity...... I am not judging; we are all subject to this and we all have made mistakes. I have been in dating relationships that I should have got out earlier and I had failed marriages. Often I wished they had left me earlier or I parachuted out, into peaceful lands. I stayed in and it was pure endurance. The clock of life moves fast, try to avoid regrets, preparing is one way this is accomplished, look at it like the script of your life, a chapter at a time, with the pursuit and hope for a happy ending. For the fairy tale to come true. Have you ever thought of the person who is struggling being homeless or dependent on drugs? how did they get there, where is there family and friends? I am sure they have or had dreams and they do have families. It is so tragic to see and to try and understand. When I see someone having a hard time and I give them some money. I have been told; do not give money they will spend it on alcohol or drugs. My conclusion is that is not a reason not to give. I look at it like this, if it gives them another day on earth, to make possible better decisions with their lives, than that is good enough. The reality is it could be us in that situation. I have owned several homes in San Diego, Portland OR, Nashville and Los Angeles. But there were times, when I had no home and I was spending nights in a car, by the beach. I have a hard time with evangelists that's state, if you give, you will get tenfold back. First it sounds like manipulation to me. Second tell that to someone in an improvised country, who lives in poverty and must go and find clean water every day. Fortunately, God does the providing ultimately, in my opinion.

Other aspect of identification is researching the company and see if there is an alignment. I think in our society we can find ourselves in a mode of compromise. Concepts like opposites attract, is not always a good idea. I have learned there are good marriage options, with people that are compatible. No one is perfect, but shared interests and working through problems is key. I think in a dating, marriage or even in work, Love and Respect can go a long way. Take this with a grain of salt or vodka, your choice. "What do I know, I am single and have been divorced", time we all get in **"Learn Mode"**. Another feature of identification is knowing what you believe at your core. An observation I am seeing, is that a lot of people are determining their beliefs or thoughts based on sound bites and tweets. They do not take the time to go below the surface, to understand what their views truly are. Emotions and hot buttons fuel their beliefs. There is no true foundation or identification to their beliefs, it is like a ship without a rudder or ship without a sail. The concern is there are subject to be influenced. History shows populations being subject to bad leadership because they were misled. Every cult always has a bit of truth mixed with lies. Okay on a lighter note. I had worked in the music industry and work in other industries and some of those were "why did I work there" jobs. I applied for a job in the IT industry, it was a major stretch for me. It was completely outside my comfort zone. What I did do, I applied everything I have mentioned in this book. There were many preliminary screening interviews. Then the big phone interview was to take place. It was a dial in Zoom type conference call, with people from all over the US. This was a new area for me, and I had never worked with IT products, completely foreign to me. I was stressed to say the least, a fish without a surf board, or something like that. What did I do? I prepared, the room I was going to take my call in. It became my canvas, my stage for the performance. I posted large diagrams, facts, and bullet points all over my walls and ceiling, I am not kidding. I studied hard and most important fact, went for it! The result was positive. They had gone through many applicants. I was now in the running for the final in person interview and it was between me and one other person. The interview was to take place in a hotel lobby in Orange County, CA an hour and a half from San Diego. I had to present and create a PowerPoint presentation to the interviewer on a technology I had no idea about. The product was thin clients that had been termed in the 1970's as a "Dumb Terminal". When I started this interview process, I was the "Dumb Terminal", but that had changed, it was time to be the expert. Excellence in everything we do, is a great thing to always strive for. In the early morning of the final interview in San Diego there were major fires all around Carlsbad near San Diego, where I lived. Smoke was everywhere, it looked like fog, but I was coughing from it, it was so bad it effected visibility. It was so horrible, I thought, and others were saying maybe you should try and reschedule the interview. There was momentum in place and I not want to disrupt it. I knew after the interview; the interviewer was flying back to his home in Utah. I went for it, got in my car to at least attempt to make it. I gave myself plenty of time to try and get there. I started to drive on the 5 freeway north toward Orange County while the fire had just jumped the freeway, now it was on both sides of the freeway. Not only was there grey smoke, but also red flames, flying high into the sky. I could feel the heat from the flames. Police and fire trucks were all around. One police car behind me started to swerve back and forth, to bring the cars behind me to a halt, so they could close the freeway down. I literally was the last car to get though before the freeway was shut down. It was a surreal feeling. Let us just say the car was running on gas and I was running on adrenaline. I had the interview and I was given the offer and it forever changed my life and my career direction. The job was representing hp (Hewlett Packard). It had been one of the best careers I had ever done. It was even better than any of my corporate music industry jobs, why because It utilized my strengths. My career involved me traveling all over the United States and Montreal. I trained hundreds of sales representatives at reseller locations. In my roles I would have meetings with CEO's, CFO's, CTO's, Directors, Presidents of large corporations in many different verticals, from healthcare to large retailers. Isn't it funny, if someone were writing a script, I would say, not possible, not believable? In summary, know you and what you stand for, surround yourself around positive people. research the companies and industries you want to work for. Prepare from the inside out. Go the extra mileS. I applied what I mentioned in this book. It never crossed my mind, that maybe I should cancel or postponed the interview. I should wait for the stars to align. I am so glad, I went for it, it changed my life. Like they say you never know unless you try, and I will repeat my quote **"Risk Equals Benefit"**! I was at the Blackjack table and I placed a bet on me for a change and it was successful. **"Bet On You and bet on those people who believe in you, they are worth some of your chips as well"**!

13

The Interview The Artificial Sweetener Not The Sugar

Think about it, how does the interviewer know you are the real deal? How do they really know you're the right fit within the companies Culture? Sure, you have a resume, references, but you control that. I often joke, one could be a full -time Interviewee, or even a Regional Interviewee, Inside or Outside Interviewee, for that matter. You get a job, based on your interview skills and that could carry you 3-to 6 months, then onto the next interview. I am going extreme, but also, I do believe they are artificial, sometimes political, and sometimes just an exercise and after the verbal obstacles an actual Offer! The main suggestion, is what we have gone through in the previous chapters, basically go to win, your A game. Easier said than done, I totally agree. That is why the pre-work is so important, plan, plan, plan so you can be you, the best you. I have gone to an interview and forgot past work information or a list of references. I would be distracted or even have left it in the car, without the opportunity to get it. I know all the cliches; you only have one first impression and guess what it is true. I usually prepare the night before, everything in one place. The suit pressed and down to polishing the shoes. Then the term "dress for success" again another truth. Sure, we may not like it, or want to go against the grain, error on the conservative, unless otherwise instructed. It is like going to a Vegas audition to be an Elvis impersonator. You are asked "What first Elvis song are you going to sing", and you reply, "Oh I don't sing Elvis songs only Nirvana songs", Next please. This is your try out or I look at it like the awkward school dance. You know, with all the nerves going, is she going to say yes or no, success or failure. If she says yes, then you must know how to dance. The difference is I don't look at an interview as a success or failure, just not the right fit or it is a great fit that will utilize your strengths. That is a cliche answer, however the interviewer really does not know you at all not to make that determination. The takeaway for me, is to know you did your best, you have checked all the boxes. Try to avoid the "Next Time, I will do that". The more you get down your process, then it becomes replication. Take care of everything that you can. This includes a professional resume. One of the best investments was hiring a resume writing company. They made it look great and put together a package also including the cover letter and thank you letter templates. Then you have a complete thought. It also demonstrates effort and care. Research top common questions that the interviewer will ask you, in the field you are applying for. Come up with answers for these questions. I would not have the answer on your phone or on a bright colored index card. "What was the question again, I have the answer, hang tight". Have questions to ask the interviewer, make sure they also apply to the context of the company and industry. It could be a one room office. "Could you tell me about your onsite gym" I have worked for companies that do have onsite gyms and restaurants but ask appropriate questions for the company within the interviewing setting. I know all this is common sense, but you would be surprised how many get some of these steps get left out. Always prepare like they are going to give you the offer. Many times I would for get one of the steps. For example, not having my list of references, with their complete information. One question I would prep for is the "Tell Me about your weaknesses", Ouch. Somehow you must burn yourself and then somehow make it positive. This is a horrible question and I have heard different responses; I don't have a great answer. My response if a customer is not happy, I can take it personally. Yeah not a good question, but I have heard it many a times. Be genuine, interested. They may also ask about a strength of yours, this is where you shine! I went to an interview for a company, that was a PR and Marketing firm in Southern California. Everyone was trendy and sat on ergonomic balls, I brought in my beach ball, but it was not to sturdy to sit on, but it was colorful. I waited in the waiting room, the waiting was like at a Doctor's office, well it did feel like that. I was not treated in a warm and fuzzy way. I went into the conference room and there were several people in there. As I walked in a girl with her cap backwards said, nice tie, basically burning me. It was done in a blatant way, they were anti-tie. Three people grilled me, and I left, thinking no way got this job. I ended getting a second interview and yes, I put on a tie again. For the record, I do not like ties. With hp no one wore ties, only a jacket, slacks and shirt and shoes. I was out of my comfort level, sure I could have dressed like them, but I was trying to be respectful. I was offered the job, I did not feel good about taking it, but I did anyway. It was not a good fit. I was the only Business Development Manager, everyone else was being trendy and coming up with trendy non applicable trendy concepts. Less than two weeks into the job, I get called into the conference room. I get presented a legal letter, with the CEO and the Office manager present. The letter stated I had 30 days to increase the sales by x amount or I would be terminated. The reason was the company had lost two major accounts, that part did not surprise me. I was still going through on-boarding training and I had the flu, that began my second day of work. I was frustrated, I had put together a sales plan together, but I was not able to present it, because I was not given the platform to do so. My first week was hearing stats and analytics and how to write the perfect email for an email blast, to a targeted market. This process included test emails to see, which one got the better response, then the email was reworked again and again, till they sounded so unnatural and pure manipulation. These creators did not even have the standard job titles, they had names like Word Smith Manager. I was given the work Title" Show Me the Cash" and I Do not Mean Johnny. Yes, I am kidding. So back to the conference room. One day the clouds parted and I could finally present my sales plan. It was thought out and virtually minimal budget was required. They loved it, and they wanted to get stared right away. A meeting was called the next day and the strategic planning was set in motion. I demonstrated the ROI (Return on Investment). After the conference meeting, I had to sign a new agreement It stated that, I still had to increase the revenue in 30 days. I replied now let me get this right, my job is the only one on the line and I am the new person. I am also the only Business Development Manager and one else here is getting this same demands I am. I resign. Let me my beach ball and my yoga mat. Goodbye! It was unrealistic and I was setup to fail. What did I learn, what I already knew, I should have never taken this job? There should be some excitement when coming on-board with a company. This job role I reported to the CEO and the President of the PR division. Her office was one door away from my office area and they are glass offices. Never once did she say hello, this is a company of less than 50 people and it is a one floor open space building. I made attempts and it would have had to take effort to avoid me. This was a toxic environment from the beginning, tension everywhere, egos running wild. The President was blunt and unfriendly, so at least she was consistent, with this company culture. It was a bad fit from the start, my gut was screaming don't do this job and my response was okay I will do it. No wonder they lost two major accounts, the monthly retainer fees they charged to their companies was shocking but, losing them came as no surprise to me. Listen to your gut, I have mentioned several times you are interviewing the company also. It is a Truth! Take the time to research and read the reviews of the company's performance and how current and past employees feel about the company and culture. I am not saying don't take chances, I did move from music business to the IT industry. But know your skill sets, those are the tools, that can allow you to cross into other vertical markets. Once your planted somewhere you need to be able to grow, this requires being firmly planted. Sometimes it is unfair or political why you don't get a job offer. I had interviewed with a well-known manufacturer of televisions. I had two interviews within the HR Department, and they went well. I was excited, he got the last interview scheduled with the Director of the Department. The second interview was by phone; I knew she was not interested right away. I went through the interview and keep trying to overcome her negative attitude. I sent follow up "thank you emails" and never heard from them again. Many times, I prepared an email to send, to show my feelings, but I stopped. Another lesson learned is to step back, before doing something harsh or abrupt. Ask yourself will it offer any benefit, will it change any minds, will you get another chance. I say this regarding work, not life. We all have learned early on that life is not always fair, and the interview process can sometimes scream this. It does not matter the company size or status. If that person ended up as my Director, it would be my living nightmare. Enterprise companies are so large sometimes, it only matters what division you're in and who you report to, A lot of the times your manager is the gatekeeper of your success or failure within the company. Not fair, tray and complain go to HR, see what changes happens. Unless this is a track record of the person, it is a losing battle. I had worked for another company, that the employees might as well been chained to our desks. We were monitored by cameras and we shared our computer screens to be monitored by the company all the work day. Now what I am about to say is true. There was also a robot, that would go up and down the aisles, also monitoring. It has a iPad looking screen and you could see the unhappy person monitoring all of us, as it patrolled the office floors. I used almost trip on this four foot robot daily. So if you read this companies reviews online, how do you think they were rated, yes that is correct! Vegas we have a winner! Why did I take this job you may ask and that is a logical question. I will quote Winnie The Pooh "I am stuffed with Fluff".

    I ran cross country in High School. I remember the prepping as you got your feet placed on the starting blocks. Then your all ready to leap and then someone jumps the gun and the process of the whole set up begins again. My nerves would be shot. We all need a great start off within a new company, so we can thrive and bring success personally and professionally to the company. Sometimes taking the high road or letting go of something is the best route. I have had many times, with interviews that were not fair, and I have had my personal pity party. One situation was with a large IT company. They were opening a new large building in Santa Monica. I thought it would be a great fit. I showed up early to the interview, an important step. Soon the reception area was filled with hopeful candidates. Being the human, I am, I was doing the comparison of those competitors for the job. The hiring managers flew in from all over the U.S to conduct these interviews. Each manger went into their own conference room. All of us applying for the jobs, would go from one to the next conference room to be interviewed by 5 interviewers. After the interviews, they would meet as a group, to go over the candidates. All of us being interviewed were outside the iron gates, hoping to get in. I felt like this was a try out for a music event. Like we spoke about in previous chapters it is like dating, yes- speed dating! First step, do we get along? Are we compatible, a good fit? Are we going to be exclusive? How many corporate kids will we have? Ok omit that question. Will it last or is there a divorce in the future. As I mentioned before the work environment is an **"At Will"** institution and I would call that the **Prenup Corporate Agreement**. Where is the snare drum hit and cymbal crash when you need it. Yes, I am making a point, the reality, principles are principles. Sometimes we make things so removed or alien to us, that we put an ocean of unnecessary obstacles in front of us. Believe me we don't need to add any additional ones to the mix. We all know the term work smart, but also observe, process, correctly and listen. Back to the interview, I made it to the next set of interviews. It ended up being between me and one other person. I decided one afternoon, to go see the latest Star Wars release for my friend's birthday. Okay he went all out. We had the big chairs and was served food at this theater. I was expecting to hear the results of the interview process, so my phone was on vibrate. I am 35 minutes into the movie, it was an intense action scene and my phone buzzes, and it is the HR recruiter. I then leave immediately from the movie theater and head to my car. The voicemail call says call,

I have some good news. In California you can't talk on the phone without an earpiece. I was a ½ hour from my home, I decided to wait and call then. I rushed into my place and I was out of breath, until I regained consciousness. I was also nervous. Her first comment was "you are hard to get a hold of". How do I answer this, throughout the whole process, I was nothing but prompt? This is one of those statements, where there is really no rebuttal. Then sorry, we offered the job to the other candidate. So, what did I do? Yes! I am the runner up, I am number two, Woo Hoo! All that work, for what! I thought, what a waste of time, this process was, I thought. I wish I never applied. The day before, I received a call from a recruiter for a television network company in Beverly Hills. He said, stand by your phone I have an offer for you. I am still standing, sleeping, and siting waiting for that call back. Yes, I have left messages, emails and nothing. I am the type of person, who analyzes everything. What could I have done different, I used to take it personal and to the extreme? I have learned to laugh about the process. Sure, it is a real experience, but they don't know if I would excel or fail at their company. I will never know the reason why, so why guess, just move on. I have broken down to the side of the road in a job pursuit process or game. There are two choices stay there or figure out how to get moving, and walk on. There is not perfect company or perfect employee, not even Vegas is perfect. I will stop on that note. Sometimes the thought of going to an interview, sounds like a dentist appointment and one would rather not do it. Your time is valuable, so it is good to assess the possible opportunity. If you have the available time, I believe it is good to interview, if the job, is something in the range of your abilities. The reason, sometimes I predetermine that a job interview is going to be unproductive and it is easy to talk ourselves out of taking that step of faith. The interview could also sound terrifying, but it is just an interview and it could be the one, you have been waiting for. Yes, it could also be a funny story, either way it is a learning experience and good practice. In Vegas the demand of interest for being part of the talent pool in a Vegas production is very competitive. Have the same tenacity as these entertainers do and usually great things will follow. Remember the interview is artificial sweetener, not the real sugar of who you are.

14

Presentation The Vegas Way

An extension of preparation and building your brand is Presentation. Las Vegas has this down. All that is needed is to look at the landscape of The Strip, this adult Disneyland, displays the hotels with a movie set appeal. Each hotel has a theme and they are paired with attractions to keep their customers entertained. Every Hotel in Vegas first has their presentation on what they have to offer. Then they present their unique portfolio of options that include entertainment, creative dining experiences, like a well-thought-out theme park. Vegas is the all included resort destination, in the middle of the desert.

Sometimes we must pay our dues, to get to our goals. I see it all the time in Las Vegas, people working two jobs, to get to their dreams. Like a vehicle, goals are the fuel that gets us there. Try and see the good in your current situations. Before a production happens, a Vegas show, a restaurant or a new apparel line is introduced to the market, there are necessary steps taken. Trend data, target market, forecasting and sometimes it is compiled in a merchandising book or some form of presentation, like a PowerPoint. Trend data, what is the current business pulse, what industries are booming, do any of these emerging or current industries line up with your goals and visions. Research the market, be engaged. Think about Vegas, it appears to effortless and it is in a lot of ways, only because of data and research. All the backstage workings of Vegas lead to the forefront with this premier presentation. Know your business, they sure do. Target markets and industries that areas you are interested in. If you are just starting your career or seasoned in your job, forecasting is key. This allows you to see where the business is currently and where it is heading in the near and distant future. We live in a world of data and sometimes it is viewed as unnecessary or boring, yet we are processing it all the time. Conclusion a traditional music teacher is not a good fit for me, but one that is open to teaching by ear, is a great fit. Sometimes we do not realize in the case of sports, I hear people rattle off stats about players, they forecast the team's season ahead, again based on statistics. In Las Vegas, many are putting their theories to the test, by gambling on it. I would ask the question "How are your stat's", "How does your next season look" and "what does your training look like". We all invest time in other interests, and nothing is wrong with that, but sometimes, we need to invest time in our stats and our future career decisions. We need to get into the mental gym and bench press until results are seen. I joined a gym recently and I had a free training session, with a workout expert. He asked me what my goals were. I have always heard people wanting a 6 pack. I used to think, why would they want beer at the gym. Yes, I am teasing. So I replied in a very serious tone, "I want a very solid 1 pack". (Can someone please get a snare drum and cymbal going). He said "give me 50 push-ups" I replied "do they still make that kind of ice cream"?

15

Degree Or Not Degree, That Is The Question

One important question is a degree necessary, that is a debate in the making. Part of preparing, selling and branding yourself is asking this question. From a personal perspective, the answer for me is, YES! Why, it is a spin at the slot machine. Hundreds of emails go before these hiring managers and based on conversations, and endless research there are certain resumes that stand out. Before that happens, many good paying jobs require it. The next fact is the candidates that have a degree are put in a separate pile than the others. The reality is you may be more qualified or do a better job, but many times you won't even get the chance to plead your case. This part is not personal, it is a process to bring down the volume of all the incoming resumes. Can you imagine receiving all the resumes and having to go through them. For that reason alone, a degree is helpful. I did not receive my degree till later in my life. I was so close to finishing it, but because of cancer, it was delayed. It really was helpful when I did complete it. It had always on my mind. I could see the finish line, but by default I took the scenic route, for many years. Today a degree can be achieved in so many ways, online, part time, while working. The degree options can also be focused and geared more toward interests. The reality is just about every industry, including entertainment prefer it and again because of the high number of applications, it is the byproduct of demand for these desirable opportunities. I don't want to sound negative, but we all have our expectations about how a career may appear or a dream of what it may be like. I love all kinds of music and I love going to concerts. As mentioned before, I have enjoyed my career in the IT industry, more than the music industry. Being around the music, apparel, and movie industry, sounds like a dream and sometimes that is true, they can also be a nightmare. I have a close friend who has had success in the movie industry, as President/Producer for a film company. For years I lived vicariously through him. My friend is extremely talented and there are perks, including financial benefits, but he can't wait to exit stage right. Now having a degree, is not the only vehicle to have you stand out. Achieving a certificate or an acquired skill certificate, can also be beneficial. In some places in the world, you chose your school metric. My ex-wife had gone the path of learning a trade in apparel, not a degree and it paid off very well for her. Acquiring achievements and accomplishments is helpful for you as a Brand and career. In the IT world certificates in technology, is extremely helpful, a BS or BA degree, a Trade certificate, are all helpful. Companies want to see accreditation, not just take your word for it. In the interview process, one other benefit of the degree is that, when someone is going through resume possibilities, a person with a college degree, jumps into the interested pile. This is better than the semi-interested pile. (Okay I am being silly now). Most company job applications I have seen and filled out have a place for where you went to college and to list your skills and certificates. Skills can also get you to the front of the line. In the IT industry, which is still a growing industry. People that have the abilities in computer programming, web development, SEO and other skills can stand out. In the music industry, having the skills in recording engineering or the understanding of the workings of the music business, like publishing, can be helpful, as well. Like I mentioned before, put the time in the research of your interests and talents. Interview yourself, ask yourself the questions, "what are my strengths? what can I do well"? A lot of times, interests we gravitate toward what we have talent in, we do not take the time to develop these natural abilities. Do an honest assessment. Everyone has a talent, sometimes we are just too close to our talent, that we assume anyone can do it, but really many times others cannot. We all have gifts and if we can take the time to identify them, they could be incorporated and embedded in your presentation. I am not saying, be self-obsessed. Gifts and talents, I believed are to be shared with others or in this case, within a career. We spoke about "AT Will" before, today's work environment is a two-way street. Interview the company as they interview you, but as we know, we also need to know our place and respect the process. After all they would be paying you and offering you benefits. I have yet to see someone get an offer, then says to the new employer, I now have an offer for you. I am not sure you would not still have the job the next day, as some kind person walks you to the door, with your belongings. Wait don't I get the window view. In certain industries, companies offer paying for courses or the ability to finish your degree. In the IT world certificates go along way and companies encourage their employees to receive them. they many times with offer this service and even provide bonuses upon completing a certificate. When we have an interest, we research it. I know we don't use that clinical term and we don't put on a white lab coat, when we are finding new music to listen to. Let's change the word to **Discovery, we all do this constantly, consciously and unconsciously.**

16

Planning The Vegas Adventure

Planning the Vegas adventure, what are you going to do when you arrive? Who will join you on your trip? If your favorite band is playing during the time your there, are you in? What if you did not prepare and the band you like, was to be there two days after you already left, suckloa! (That sucks-translated). Yes, I make up words. The point is this process comes natural for us. What is important, it does take effort but it is enjoyable effort. Sometimes, it is hard to get it going, our personal engine won't start. We need to be jumped started! It is like when you have a paper due for school, Procrastination sets in. For me it used to be avoidance at all costs. Then the storms of the paper deadline starts coming. My engine also starts and my foot is heavy on the accelerator. The paper gets done, fueled by coffee and Red Bull. Then there is a sense of satisfaction. Applying **"Learn Mode"**, it is all about steps being taken for **"YOUR END GOAL OR GOALS"**. Getting a paper turned in , may seem trivial in Your big picture. It is like a brick to add to the bridge to get you there. **"Small Tasks Lead To Big Accomplishments"**. Most things in life take time. For example a good wine, involves many steps. The development of a song, from conception to production, to distribution. Now that it is pointed out, stay in the natural mode. Since it is what we do, with our day to day interests. Then try applying it to our job day, yes sometimes they are long days, but it takes the same effort to **"Tune Out as It Does To Tune In"** , find your favorite radio channel in your head and it will help you see the exciting goal destination, in your near future. I speak from first-hand experience, I used to wing it for a job interview, for example. The reason was not apathy, but terror and fear. If I don't think about it, it will happen in a positive way, fingers crossed. Those long walks to the company building, then to the front office gate keeper, glancing at the name of the person I am meeting with, so I pronounce it correctly. I thought about every step, every single moment. The bottom line, I want to be accepted and liked, not rejected. I would guarantee a performer in Vegas, before they go on stage, hopes they are well received. I don't think they say, "I hope I suckola tonight". I can't understand when people say, "Break a leg", as if that is a positive uplifting comment. Most hear that and don't respond. What should you say in response, "Maybe I will break both legs "and don't forget to smile, when responding, be positive. (lol) It is like you are going into the interview and someone says "I hope you stumble on your words" of course they would mean it in the most uplifting way. I hope they don't say that at the acrobat shows in Vegas. Someone is about to propel about as high as the clouds. Hey, "Break a leg" , in return from the acrobat, from mid-air a middle finger is returned, of course with the best intentions and a smile. Okay I will stop now, onward. The point is preparation and planning are necessary for a career but leaving room open is also good. You also need to breathe and let the natural you be present. Remember that preparation, sets the stage for a natural outcome. We have spoken throughout these chapters to plan, so the natural you comes out. Also planning and being prepared, lets you respond quickly if there are glitches. When planing for a concert, our band would have to unload the equipment and set the stage up. It would take several hours to plug in the cables and do a sound check. One concert I will never forget happened the Redondo Beach Civic Theater,in Southern California. This concert had bad planning from the start. It was to be a sold out concert. We had to have a guest sound engineer for that night. We rushed to setup and we got it done, just as people took their seats. We all had a sigh of relief, as we started tuning our guitars. Because people were seated , we could not do a sound check. I will never forget it, our engineer was high above the balcony in a glass sound proof room. He looked like he was in an aquarium. The lights went out as we got on stage, then the music started as the spot lights hit us. Our music was extremely loud , my vocal microphone was feed-backing, as the sound came from our stage monitors. I looked out in the audience and the people looked confused, usually they are standing and moving. I was always moving on the stage and I walked toward the crowd and there was no sound coming from the main theater speakers only from the monitors on stage. The sound engineer forgot to plug in the main sound speakers, this is a fairly large arena with several thousand seats and it was sold out. Oh when I had been looking up, he looked busy, sliding dials and adjusting who knows what. It was three songs in before we had it corrected. I was so embarrassed, we were not upset. The show must go on! Not being rushed, last minute prepping, causes these things to happen. Then there was a dance we were playing for on a military base. We were in our band bus, that was ready to break down at any moment. Yes, we were running late. So we were speeding on the military base to get to the dance hall. Then we got pulled over for speeding by the military police. The ticket cost more, than we probably got paid. We finally got setup and began the concert. I forget how many songs we had played, when coming from my bass speaker cabinet was the sounds of a helicopter and the pilot communicating with dispatch. It is hilarious thinking about it now . Then I felt like we were recreating Pink Floyd "The Wall", which for the record is one of my favorite records. The point of the story is we could have avoided the ticket if we were not running late. However the helicopter sounds and conversations , they would have still happened. **Plan so you, can expect the unexpected!**

17

Vegas is Always Changing So Should We

Two songs and the artists that come to mind, are archived in my rock file, Reo Speed Wagon and the sounds of David Bowie. The band I was in high school, many Saturday mornings in my friends (The Drummers) garage. We would we jam and attempt to recreate these and other favorite band songs, we had a blast, the neighbors and the community as whole, well that was questionable. I remember sometime after we stopped as a band. A girl from school said to me " I am so glad that band stop playing on the weekends, it used to wake me up and my family, we could not find where the noise was coming from, did you ever hear them". She really did not have a clue I was in that band, I replied, without missing a beat "No, but it must have been awful", she replied, "It was the worst". The funny part was the community was in canyons and it provided great reverb and the sound traveled and bounced around. It would be hard to pinpoint where the sound was coming from, our band was Stealth. Change is the thought. We always should be in a mode of change and hopefully for the better, avoid the negative counterpoint. As with everything in life something that is positive, can have the negative counterpart. In the positive way, modification and learning what works and what does not work is helpful. It is like making a recipe and you follow the instructions to the "T, but the last 10% is ad-lib. You decide to leave out the sugar and this dessert, it is not so tasty, is the result.

Brand you, know you, prepare you, change-adapt and invent or reinvent you. There is no better place to look at for change than Las Vegas. The beginnings were Fremont & Main Street, back in the 40's, now it is "The Strip", lined with high rise hotels, themes and attractions. The historic part of Vegas is being revamped, but like historic sites of Rome, there are relics that still stand, to show the history of Vegas. They say if the IT world and all the innovations, were to stop, it could lead to a major depression. Change can be a positive thing and knowing the history of where you have been and where you are today and where you are going is a good assessing tool. Change does not always mean complete renovations or transformations; it can just be minor modifications or tweaks. The people that has graced the stages in Vegas for example Sinatra, Sammy Davis Jr. Elvis Presley, Marilyn Monroe and the list goes on. There are also the new artists that perform in Vegas today, is it better today? The point is you could say the technology is better, state of the art sound systems, Larger music arenas, more ways to market, like digital signage, online. However, talent is timeless, the way the talent is presented, marketed, prompted and delivered is subject to change and improve. Look at how music is recorded, it used to be done in an analog format with reel to reel tapes. Now it is digital and much easier to record and with less of a budget. Now ad the latest technology great songs, books and other art forms can be digitized and preserved. Have you ever seen a band you like, record new music and it is completely different from their last record, like another band and you don't get it? Sometimes that can work, or other times it is risky. Not to get to philosophical, but we all can do this at some point. We are chasing after something; a career path and we lose ourselves along the way. The reality is **"You Can't Run Away From You"**! When I got divorced the first time, my ex-left me and I was devastated to say the least. She was there for me during my cancer treatments and I was with her as she had successes in the apparel industry. We moved around to many states in the U.S for her to continue with her success. Sure, we benefited financially and owned many homes and lived in beautiful areas, but was I fulfilled and happy, not at all. Would I have made a lot of different decisions, if I could do it all over, Yes! Did I spend years going over and over, the what if scenarios? Yes! If this happened my life would be like this. The result is it was all a waste of time. During those years I did change, I did make modifications and the result was an ineffective shell of a person, I was defeated. The one thing that does not stop is time and it is the most valuable commodity. Yes, we ultimately had nice things and material comforts and I was thankful for them, but like many, I would trade it all in for peace, love, respect and happiness. After the divorce, I had to learn to live with me alone again. I really did not want to spend time with myself during those days. I had fallen so far down the slopes of life, to the point I did not recognize myself. But we are now getting along just fine now. Know your strengths and weaknesses, change, modify only when necessary. We all don't succeed at everything, we all make mistakes, but we should try and learn to be better. Don't beat yourselves up and try not to allow the despair cloud your life. Look at it, take the lesson or value from the situation and move toward your goals. Then look in rear view mirror, wave it goodbye, sometimes we flash the middle finger, but just let it go. "**Avoid The Repeat Cycle**", you now are already **Clean!** If I were to analyze the medical costs during my cancer treatments, it is mind blowing. My insurance ran out early and I was helped with government programs, for which I am truly thankful. The reality though is there are always bills that followed us for long time. Each of my surgeries I was told were $350, 000 and I had it done twice. Then the Chemotherapy drugs were up to $12,000 each and there were 22 of them and then there was the hospital stays, my home away from home. First, looking at all these expenses, I thought I was wealthy on paper and it all went away. I thought about all the vacations, that that money could be used for and the guitars I could buy, you can never have to many, right? Then I realized that I was rich beyond all measure because I could breathe and live, thank you God! For me I realized I really do not own anything, everything is on loan to me. When I owned homes, I had mortgages, the house was on loan to me and my car , but I had a false sense of ownership. The saying goes "you can't take it will you," it is true. I heard recently a story of a man was going to pass away and he wanted all his money put into the casket when he passed away, his wife agreed. Before the casket was closed, she did what was requested and she placed, the money in the casket. Her friend said, "that was incredible how you honored his last request", she replied "Yes, I wrote a check for the entire amount". What a true statement, you don't take it with you and he will not be cashing that check anytime soon. Now I believe there is nothing wrong with making money and working hard and having the benefits from it. Do also things that allow for positive changes. Take more classes , read more, play more and remember sometimes take the **"Risk equals Benefit"**!

18

The Offer, The Contract

The Corporate hurdles have been jumped. In any business, a contract/agreement is presented, and this applies to Vegas as well. If you are involved with the company, the contract will stand. In the past, this step has been a real weakness of mine. I can negotiate for others and be clear, precise and provide intelligent advice. With me I turn off the logic switch and switch completely to the emotional side. Buzz words like Music Industry, I am, foaming at the mouth. "This is a "100% commission and no benefits", well that sounds great! I might reply. Part of this process is knowing your weaknesses and compensating to move that to a strength position. I spoke about being an athlete, growing up. I swam, ran, skateboarded, body-boarded, skied, coach soccer and more. Many times, on a business trip, I would hear from work associates, "how's it going gimpy" referring to my leg and my limp. Oh, the responses that I wanted to say back with, they were creative statements, but I never responded. Those statements could at times, cause me to stumble, and fall and feel insecure and miss the things I could do in my past. What I have learned is to focus on what I can do and what I can change and discard and bypass those hurtles. It is always a choice for me to internalize that pain. In the music business in the past the record deals were notorious and in favor of the record labels and the corporate castles in the hills of Hollywood and Santa Monica. Bands shut off the logic and operated in the feel-good mode, which like alcohol happy in the moment and the next day, the headache and the I will never drink again mode sets in. Funny we all have the amnesia, effect, because we are prone to repeat that pattern . again, if not careful. When a company presents an agreement/contract you have entered the honeymoon period, use that as a benefit to you. Just like a relationship, work together. Get it all in writing, request a day or two to review the agreement. Seek counsel from people who are close to you and a key factor, they may have better business sense than you, at the time because they are removed. Do yourself and find someone who is objective and will not automatically agree with you. Recently I helped a friend get a large-dollar base increase at a new company over her last employer, then there were commissions/bonuses on top of that. She originally talked herself out of even interviewing for the role, that would have been a big mistake. Her last job, she was making great money and to bump up the new offer amount of money, even better. She had been getting a lot of interviews, but equal amount of rejections. I enjoyed helping her prep and prepare for the interviews and the result it paid off. Part of me after our effort wanted the job. It was a Brand Evangelist role for a Large healthcare organization. It was classified as a sales position, that is a stumbling block for many, as we have discussed. We have also explored in this book, that sales has many aspects to the term and even more stigmas. She is thriving in the job and is growing in this role. I think the lesson we can learn, is go outside your comfort zone. A fresh perspective helps. I have over the years, developed, and discovered areas of strengths and weakness in the field of sales. When employers are advertising today, they use terms like "hunter, prospector, cold caller". In school over the years I heard about early settlers, being termed Hunters and Gatherers. They never post are you a sales "Gatherer". The way I look at a "Gatherer" is they gather information. Who is there ideal customer, what is the customers' needs and wants, and understanding their pain points? This is a term called "Solution Selling", it is really putting the customer first. This is not the approach of a Customer Service role, that is more reactive. This is understanding the customer in a proactive manner and bringing the proper solution. It is being honest with an infusion of integrity and bottom line customer care. I have done the cold calling, smile and dial approach and I suck at it. Trying to push unnecessary products, that the person does not even want. Being customer first focus, means, sometimes your product you represent is not the right choice. That message also needs to be communicated. When I represented hp, I had my product lines. When I met with a CEO , I would try and align them with my product solution. To get to that appointment the due diligence would have needed to have taken place first. But if for some reason my product was not a good fit, I would have another hp direction. I would direct them to the correct person or team. member that represented the solution needed. I realized that, that if the customer is happy, then naturally I will also be happy from the closed business. The second benefit is called retention. A satisfied customer will stay with you for their next order to be placed. If I were a Sales Manager of people, I would fail. People say I am a people person, but I would not be good at managing them. Now managing product, product training speaking, managing trade show booths, I think is a good fit. It does involve people, but it is almost subtle the difference, but day to day, they could not be more different and light years apart. Then comes work ethic. Here are some thoughts. Work hard, be involved, do extra, be helpful and participate. One lesson I have learned about helping, is know exactly what that means, have it clearly defined. I was in process of relocating for a company, to represent the South-East Region, before I covered the Western Region. I agreed to helping out a co-worker at an event in Texas. I was in route to Nashville and I was in Oklahoma. I had to board my dog and board a flight to get there. I was trying to communicate by email and phone, just the normal confirmation process. When I arrived in Texas, they had an issue with my rental car, they ran out of them, that was the first hiccup. I took a cab, rushed in, to find my speaking engagement was canceled and TBD ,when it was to be rescheduled. The Senior Sales Representative for the reseller was having a nervous breakdown. I had traveled two weeks earlier to the reseller's location and she had hives from the stress. At that point I was the hero, saving the day, by my wiliness to help. I heard her put down her company and team members. She was extremely negative and vocal about it. It was so bad, if anyone there heard it, she would have been fired on the spot. The trip just got worse and worse. That night was a dinner event, the entertainment was a Armadillo race, yes you heard right to be followed by a square dance. It was as bad as it sounds, all I could think about was rescuing the Armadillos and getting out of there. This cost me time and the company travel expenses and I was set up to fail. The end result, I was the scapegoat. I was told someone had to be blamed for the event. Since I was leaving the region, I was the target an easy target. It was completely political and I was hurt. All I wanted to do was help a team member out. Hindsight, I think the person I helped knew what was ahead and he opted out. In the discussions that followed ,they did not go well. The lesson I learned is it is okay to say no. Being a team player, does not mean, you are the fall person. There is nothing wrong with looking out for your best interests, remember you must think about your family, which could translate to even your pets, which are family members. You should take care of you. Giving is good, but giving back to you, allowing yourself to recharge is best for the company and all involved. I have seen this happen before, when someone does something outside their scope of work or in a different department and it goes wrong. The response usually is not, "I know you were only trying to help", no you are full invested, the second you signed up. I have spent time on this because it can be commonplace. There are people in the work setting, that spend all their time blaming other people and not taking responsibility for their own actions. If there is an issue, they will send an email, to cover themselves. Sometimes it is almost like the entire company directory will get copied on that email. It would be like an actor who has the lead in a musical in Vegas and cannot go on because of laryngitis. Someone backstage says "I got this" I will cover him. He goes on, it is a sold-out night. He does not know the lines, or the songs and he is does not sing. It is a painful performance. The curtains come down.

In summing up these thoughts, in your agreement/contract, it is usually very clear on your responsibilities for your position with the company. Try and stay within those guidelines, when I do, it can prevent possible negative situations. There are only so many hours in the day, your time is valuable. There needs to be the work life balance. I have learned this lesson finally and as I mentioned throughout this book it is "AT WILL" the two words that caused my revelation. There is no longer, work for the corporation for 30 years and retire with benefits. The employer can terminate the working agreement at any time for any reason. But it continues that the employee can leave for any reason with no adverse consequences. **Work hard, but also Work Smart!**

19

Daydreaming About Vegas

Dreaming is something I am good at, daydreaming even better. The only problem I have is I never received a paycheck for it, yet.... But I can still dream about it. Many people have dreamed of their visions people like Walt Disney, Richard Branson, Elon Musk and Steve Jobs and then there was that movie "Field of Dreams" with the famous quote "Build it and they will come". That is a true statement, but there are key components with the term "**Build**". This requires a plan, tools, a blueprint, a map, research, commitment, dedication, a sales plan and much more. Vegas has followed this kind of strategy. What is unique about Las Vegas, it is always improving, modifying, and expanding. We all see the world differently and we definitely all have personalities and amazingly we are all created differently. I really do not think any two people are identical in thoughts or appearance. That is why there are many different music styles, car options, apparel choices, living choices and where to live choices. Think about some people choose to live in a cold climate and some in the warmth near a beach. It is all about choices, everything is and even if you don't want to make one, by default a choice is made, we see this all the time in life.

I have heard people proclaim, it is hopeless, and I cannot change. It does not have to be labeled change, call it growth. Like learning to ride a bike or to drive a car. When I had my permit, my dad drove with me to the DMV, to get my driver's license. I was so nervous, and my driving was reckless, that day. and every other day. My dad remained calm. Around two blocks from the DMV, not sure how I did it, but I drove up and over a middle grass divider, facing ongoing traffic. It must have looked comical in how that was done. My dad calmly said I think we will go home now; you won't be going to get your license today. I laugh today, he was not even upset through the experience. The next time we went, 10 years later and I was good to go. It was a week later really. The work environment is competitive out there; we all have grown up around that concept. School and sports are just two examples. It is funny how we all can forget the subtle aspects of life. If you were to break it down, human nature does not change much. Think back to your school days and as painful as it could have been or not been. There is the school structure. There were the popular students, yes there are the popular ones in the workplace, the Stuck-Up ones, oh yeah them also, The Jerks, checked that box. The Bullies, The Cheaters, The Slackers, and the list go on. The positive list is the Smart ones, The Effective ones, you get the idea. All the playground did was change the environment to **"The Corporate Playground"** (I plan to write a book about this and that will be the title), but some still operate the same way. Maybe I am over simplifying, but there is some truth here. Some people continue, if they are allowed, to bring their fraternity ways with them. I have witnessed and have seen the blatant and undercurrent of corporate bullying. Compromise, employers or employee's deciding their own form of ethics or moral code. This time the stakes are higher and have a bigger price tag. Decisions made in the corporate world, the scandals ruins careers and entire families lives. I have known and seen the fallout many life changing events, that have taken place at sales retreats and other meetings. Executives asked to step down due to discretionary events. The positive side is we can make our own story and remove the chaos and drama and receive the peace that follows. There are always two sides to life, every Spider-man, Superman, Star Wars movie, there is the villain and sometimes they show up in the work place. When researching the companies, you are interested in, do the preparing. Try to remove any emotion to add bias to the process and be as objective as you can. In the past I tended to romanticize a job or company, especially if it was related to the music industry or something of interest. I was so desperate at those points in my life, that if the job description said, "great opportunity, so good, you pay us to work here". I would have considered it. My work aspiration bubbles have been popped and about time. I have moved across the country for an opportunity that seemed good to me. I had even been given, great advice, why not to make the move, but I went anyway. I became desperate and wanted a quick fix. Some were good jobs, but in the wrong market and once there it was impossible to move to a better fit position, within the same company. This happened to me with a large radio network, that has a huge presence yearly in Las Vegas. After I had been laid off from a company. I was in 5th gear and I became desperate. In a short period of time, I moved from Nashville, to Oklahoma, the Colorado, Florida and California. I now joke "50 states in 50 months". I was not laughing then. My second job was a relocation specialist. Here is the worst part, none of these moves had a relocation package, it was all out of my own pocket. This is difficult to admit, truth is sometimes hard to look at. Many people have ridiculed me and basically said I was in essence dumb, in decision making. Hindsight is the rear-view mirror of life. It can teach us something, but in is not a place you want to dwell in. Oh, I have spent time in Hindsight City. Whenever I drive out of Las Vegas, I experience the rear-view phenomenon. While in Vegas, no I am not thinking, while in Rome.... While in Vegas, it is larger than life. The replica of the Eifel tower with Paris Paris, feel like the real, Eifel tower, I have been to both. This is really expressed when looking up at the tower from the pool. Although I don't remember the pool around the Eifel tower in Paris., I must have missed that. The experience while driving away is it begins to fade into the surrounding desert. Miles of cactus, dry land, as Vegas fades away, like a mirage. Even when you fly out of Vegas, I get that same experience, it is there and then it is gone. Oh, now that is a topic for discussion. I think about all musical geniuses lost recently and in the past. We have also lost the geniuses in the IT world, as well. There lights have faded into the desert, but their legacy will continue to spark the inspiration of others. This is why I wrote this book. Not to say, look I have it all figured out. Do my 1, 2,3 steps and you have a million dollars in the bank and a dream career. What is so positive is knowledge and learning is free. I know of a band that is part of the same organization of ASCAP, that I am. People told him to give up his music dreams and get a life basically. he was broke,about to get kicked out of his apartment and his reply was I only have a Plan A, I have no other back up plan. Plan A worked for him and he is still highly successful artist and songwriter. With all the advice, and decisions are made, opportunities taken or not taken, will shape you and me. The way we view ourselves is what matters. Be your best fan, no matter what! cheer yourself on. Root for you! I spoke about being in my 20's and being diagnosed with osteosarcoma and my odds of survival was very low percentage. It was all about survival. My second chemo OD my body and had no white count and I had a high fever and an infection of my own body was shutting down. This was my second drug and 20 more to go over a year and a half more. I was put in a germ-free room, no one was allowed in. I knew I was close to death, I felt helpless and I was scared, to say the least. Do you think I thinking, I can't wait to get on stage and perform with a great record deal? How I am going to climb the corporate ladder with these, crutches? I did not feel like a man, I was a scared child. My family and close friends were there, but there was a world between us. I felt alone and in despair. During that time, so much happened, that is would take a complete book to express. All my prior investments in dreams, sacrifices, dedication, came to one-word now survival. The momentum and the sense, I am right there, I could taste the rewards, of efforts. It all came to a complete stop and not a temporary stop, as far as my focused career path, it was completely gone, it, like it never existed. I tried for years and years to find that path again, and those were my wilderness years. I knew I was close to death then. One night the head of oncology, went against the orders and came into my germ-free room, she kissed me on the lips and brought me flowers. Both are not good things. Germs from even a kiss was dangerous and flowers with no immune system is also dangerous. She said you must fight, your soldiers (referring to my white blood count) losing the battle, if you give up. No drug could have boosted my courage up, like she did. Many of the other Doctors treated me like I was already gone. She brought me a huge dose of hope and love. Do not underestimate this power, called encouragement! This power also is not seen in a paycheck, we all can be rich with love if we invest in mind, body and soul. I began to slowly improved. I was in the hospital for a long time. Fast forward, when the tumor was removed and it was 100% dead, that was a miracle. The way my body was hit then, later it was a blessing. God had displayed is grace and love to me. Yes, a 100% dead and it was 100% God in my opinion. Life can be fragile we will spend most of our lives in school and then work. How we live our lives at home intersects on how we live our lives at work. The famous line don't bring your work home with you. Yeah right. Everything we do affects everything. At work we make the money to pay, the mortgage, the kid's schoolbooks, keep the food and lights on. Another gambling win in Vegas to bet on, that every marriage has had the conversation topic of money, I then would be extraordinarily rich. As mentioned, before it is all about universal choices, that all blend together and in turn makes us who we are as a person. (We cannot separate it. I am a work in progress when it comes to life. I try to see the positives in every decision I make. I am not being naive in that respect, in other areas, I can be. I have made friends at each place I had worked at. I received sales and marketing training's from the best of the best companies. I have not only friends but business opportunities from these jobs. I lived in great locations, on the beach in Florida, one exit away from garden of the gods, the most amazing trails, and mountains in Colorado Springs. I have lived by the ocean in Southern California, with my daily walk, a cup of coffee on the cliffs, looking down on the sea. Yes, bad business decisions on a resume, but the resume of life, not bad. At least I took chances and I tried, A for effort, right? Stepping outside your comfort zone, can be a good thing sometimes. The notion, that the grass is greener, over at that company is not always the case. The reality is your exchanging one set of problems for another. Sometimes I think about a interview setting, how I must navigate through my resume without offering shot of their favorite liqueur and one or two for me as well? The trail of my past resume is like the map to find buried treasure. Like where is Waldo, it is Where has Brian gone now. I wrote a song called **"What We Did Wrong"** one line in the song is **"feel like I lived in every state, just trying** hard **to contemplate what I did wrong, what we did wrong"** . It is true after being laid off from work and the end of a marriage. I went through a long period of disappointments. I thought I would have had children; we were close with a ectopic and a miscarriage pregnancy. My life was totally different from how I imagined it would be. I have had to get to know me and spend time with me at times in my life when I did not want to be near me but escape or run away from me. I hope you can learn from my mistakes and avoid them in your career and life. But when you make mistakes, I hope you learn from them and can grow as a person. Here is a thought, those who read this book, let's try and meet sometime in the future in Las Vegas and share our stories, in the oasis in the desert, where people dream and make dreams come true. We all go through the deserts of life, but the water and lights are closer than you think. There is luck at the tables in Vegas but life it takes a bit more than just that.

I have always dreamed big and I have always wanted to help and encourage others. In the past I had the taste of success. I believe there is a positive aspect to success. In life and the circumstances that come along the way, dreams can also modify and change. I still dream big, but I look through different eyes. Before I thought about doing my music in front of large audiences and being well received, after my life changing experiences. My focus was now hoping I could encourage just one person in this world. If one person is touched or inspired by my music, I am happy and fulfilled. Then I view that as success. If more like it, then that is icing on the cake! Try not to let anyone define success for you. It has been freeing, people have responded all over the world with my music. Could I produce the music better, with more of a budget, sure. It is not about that, it is about a connection, filtering through the chaos of life and finding a common thread, that weaves us all together. The pursuit to try and take the garbage from this world recycle it and create hope and something beautiful, now that is a dream. I want to work for a dream, not for just a paycheck. That is the true riches to me. My resume has been a disaster, but here are some highlights, taken from my resume. Because of a job, I was able to spend many hours with Johnny Cash and June Carter Cash, yes, we talked guitars and music. I helped promote records for Joe Strummer (The Clash), Roland Orzabal (Tears for Fears), Dolly Parton, Glen Phillips (Toad the Wet Sprocket), John Waite (The Baby's) and Journey which by the way was the first concert I had ever saw. I promoted a Canadian band that opened for Paul Rodgers of Bad Company, spent time with him in San Diego and then with him backstage at the Fillmore in San Francisco. One fond memory was during my chemotherapy time, I sang back up on a Christmas compilation record to raise money for pediatric cancer with Commodores. I had no hair and skin and bones, but I was smiling, and they were very gracious and welcoming. Years later, I had a temporary job with Taco Bell Corporation at their high-rise building in Irvine. One morning I was walking in the lobby and they were displaying a video and I glanced at it. It turned out they were sponsors of this Pediatric Cancer Christmas record. There I was singing back up with the Commodores, without hair and on crutches. I cannot explain the emotions I felt, let's just say I have tears in my eyes again while I write this. I was then in a moment transported back to all the memories. I had to step outside to regain composure at the time. I did not share that moment with anyone there, that was for me only. I mention this exhaustive narrative, because all this happened post cancer period in my life. As mentioned earlier Donny Osmond and his manager Bill opened the door when I was feeling hopeless and very discouraged. Before Donny's help, a lot of bubbles were popped, I was disillusioned and had lost hope. One attempt I had gone into a friends recording studio, to record some songs I had written. I was terrified, my voice was now different, from the surgery. The result was not bad. I put together a very nice package, with my bio and demo. I was excited to share my new music. I did not use my cancer experience in my bio, it was just the music. One song on that demo was called "What Really Matters is Love" one line is "broken bridges you need to cross, but you can't cause of fear" I sent it off to many record labels. This demo was geared toward the Christian market. With a spark of inspiration and hope as I dropped them in the mailbox. Generic rejection letters came, and more bubbles got burst. Yes, I was heartbroken, I wanted to get a PA system and a Mic and shout, do you know what it took to do this!. In the past, I played many gigs, where thousands of people showed up. It was energizing and exciting. The reality is the show ends, the crowd leaves and I would leave alone. The rejection letters seemed cold, but I understood. One response was different to me. I was sent a personal letter from a major Christian producer. It was a long letter, full of examples of how he can't listen to my demo, because he is so busy and then he signed it. I just found the letter. I was taken back then and even today. With the amount of time spent, displaying his importance, he could have put the tape in the player and wrote back saying that was "terrible". That I would have respected. I released a song called "Can't Rewind". One line is "what about the days of glory". I would fly out to Nashville for many years to the GMA week, Gospel Music Week. I wanted so bad to be back and pick up where I left off. It never happened. I cannot sum of the sadness and despair I felt. I was still young. Yes, I have confused employers that have interviewed me, with lines from them saying things like "Now let me get this right" as they try to navigate through my resume obstacle course. Next time I will quote this famous statement modified for me. "What Happens in Brian (Vegas), Stays in Brian(Vegas)" . Now in an interview I smile, and I own my resume and state "this is my journey". Yes it is turbulent like the flight into Vegas, but it is an exciting journey.

    One thing I find humorous is where companies have their meetings. They are always at amazing locations. This concept begins early on when we were in school. I remember growing up in Southern California and living near Disneyland. School would have a field trip there and all the students would be excited, until we got there. No, we did not get to ride the Matterhorn or Space Mountain. We saw a side to Disneyland we never knew existed. It was like being a fish in an aquarium looking at the ocean, beyond the glass. The business events I attended as an adult would be literally in front of a major ski lifts at a major resort, Disneyland, Vegas, Orlando, California (Los Angeles, San Francisco, and San Diego). Like the school field trips, it was an exercise in frustration. 95% work and 5% free time. I often wondered if there was some psychology behind this, either conscious or subconscious.

20

How To Get To Vegas

(Detour In Miami)

There are many ways to get to Vegas, but It takes planning for an excursion to Vegas. We all shop for a good deal on an airline ticket, rental cars and hotels, it all gets mapped out. Throughout this book we talk about branding, marketing, sales and what is a great fit, from a career point of view. What better picture than planning a trip to see these all features come together. First seen is what is familiar the brand, all the recognized names of airlines, hotels, car rental places. Then comes marketing, discounts and offerings associated with the brands. Then the combination is how are they going to sell you. If you stay at our hotel, you will have a luxurious sparkling pool, with trendy people laying out by the pool or whatever their approach is. How are you going to get your dream career? One is to learn your craft, do something every day toward your goal. Read, interview with people doing what you are interested in, intern and volunteer. Rarely do things happen by osmosis. We all hear of people winning large amounts of money in Vegas and then soon they have spent all the money and we all say we would not do that. Without research on investing and how to handle money, we sure could. So, understand the wise approach's with money, it is still wise to understand how to keep it and how to increase it better yet. Usually everything is somewhat of a struggle, before success happens, only the degree of it is the variable. We are getting close to the end of the book, but not the end of the unwritten chapters, you all have inside of you! I have

HOW TO GET A JOB VEGAS STYLE

mentioned several times, my motto **"Risk Equals Benefit"** . It comes down to choices to get to Vegas and when you arrive in Vegas. I have lived my motto, the last few years and for years now. I had been spending my time recently in Clearwater and Miami. It was a very difficult time, but also amazing. I spent time staying in hostels, something I had never done before. I met amazing life long friends, from Argentina, Ireland, Slovakia, Australia and a great friend from Sweden, now in Colombia. I was also going out with the girl of my dreams from Colombia, she always takes my breathe away because she is beautiful ,but the most beautiful aspect, is her is her beautiful heart! My times knowing her was like a dream, but in January 2020 on my birthday she broke up with me. We were close, we had looked at engagement rings and the main reason I stayed in Florida was it is very bilingual. I made several trips to see her there. The first trip no one knew, except a music producer that I work with, that I was going. I was so nervous and I got so lost trying to find the hotel where we were going to meet at. For me seeing her in person was magical, yes a dream come true! She is always on my heart and her family has a special place there as well! Yes my heart still breaks, but I have no regrets at all to taking steps of faith and completely opening my heart to her. Yes there was **Risk, but worth it!** and Yes there was **Benefit,** I got to spend time with a beautiful princess and show my love, **for my forever Princesa en Rosa!** The times that followed afterward were very difficult and if I am honest they still are. On that Valentines Day, I saw couples in Miami all around me celebrating. I watched the Pink and Blue sunset and dreamed I was with her, as I laid on the beach all night. Pink is her favorite color and Blue is mine. I have a new song, soon to be released called , can you guess "Pink and Blue Skies". For this song, I will write out all the lyrics.

Your in my heart my love and I am always here for you

Never felt this way before, your love has always gotten me through

Pink and Blue Skies, Light up the night, they always remind me of me and you
Pink and Blue Skies, Lost in your eyes, Juntos mi amor, simepre aqui para ti

Feels like forever, on the shores of my desires

Don't know what to do, please come and light the fires of love

Pink and Blue Skies, Light up the night, they always remind me of me and you
Pink and Blue Skies, Lost in your eyes, Juntos mi amor, simepre aqui para ti

Tienes mi corazon , espero en las orillias , hemos visto todavia creo

Juntos en amor, simepre aqui para ti

The nights are fading fast, will our love last, storm are approaching

hold on tight to our memories in flight, try to fly above all pain that is in sight

Pink and Blue Skies, Light up the night, they always remind me of me and you
Pink and Blue Skies, Lost in your eyes, Juntos mi amor, simepre aqui para ti

21

Playing Slots Time

When I sit down playing slots, I like to observe people. That could be a book topic alone. As I mentioned earlier the flight in my experience has always been turbulent flying into Vegas. The good part is you then land and get off the plane. Like this book, some has been smooth sailing and yes some has been turbulent messaging. I have enjoyed this time we have spent together, and I hope, there is some take a way's, that you find helpful. There is no magic message or 1,2,3 steps to secure your business destination. There is however the ability to learn from my mistakes, avoid mistakes and ways to recover and reinvent yourself. We all need a toolbox that includes all the essential tools, but what we build and create comes from each of us as individuals. The true purpose is to have the platform to express your ideas and concepts and display your gifts and talents. It is taking all the steps needed for your audition in Vegas or wherever your Vegas is in this world. Success is measured ultimately by you and it is much bigger than the status or work title on your business card. It is the contributions and choices you make for You, for your family, friends and the world as a whole.

I am excited where I am now in my journey, I am a Partner with an IT company in the AI technology (Artificial Intelligence) space. I have started to launch my apparel company, called audiolution TM. (www.audiolution.com). I am writing new music with my band

Phonoville, (www.phonoville.info) and I have other ventures soon to be announced.

My hope is whoever takes the chance and reads this book. If you would like to meet and discuss what you have learned, I am in. My proposal is we all try and meet in Vegas sometime. I will be there, I am already applying the suntan lotion, who will take me up on this offer. This is extended to all. I hope you enjoy this book as much as I have enjoyed writing it. Please reach out. Much Success, fulfillment, and most of all peace! Viva Las Vegas!!!

Brian Waters is currently a Partner with Clear Sky Technologies an AI "Artificial Intelligence" company. He was an English Major at UCLA and received a BA degree in Liberal Arts from Concordia University, Irvine CA. He is President/Owner of audiolution ™ an apparel brand and music platform company. Brian has an entrepreneur spirit and also song writes for his band Phonoville and other artists.

www.ingramcontent.com/pod-product-compliance
Lightning Source LLC
Chambersburg PA
CBHW071407290426
44108CB00014B/1716